PATHS TO
RUSSIA

PATHS TO RUSSIA

FROM WAR TO PEACE

by F. WILHELM CHRISTIANS
CHAIRMAN, SUPERVISORY BOARD, DEUTSCHE BANK

Foreword by HELMUT SCHMIDT
FORMER CHANCELLOR OF WEST GERMANY

Translation from the German by
Joachim Neugroschel

Macmillan Publishing Company   New York
Collier Macmillan Canada   Toronto
Maxwell Macmillan International
New York   Oxford   Singapore   Sydney

Macmillan Publishing Company
866 Third Avenue, New York, NY 10022

Collier Macmillan Canada, Inc.
1200 Eglinton Avenue East, Suite 200
Don Mills, Ontario M3C 3N1

Library of Congress Cataloging-in-Publication Data
Christians, F. Wilhelm.
  Paths to Russia: From War to Peace / by F. Wilhelm Christians ;
  introduction by Helmut Schmidt.—
  English translation ed.
    p. cm.
  ISBN 0-02-525241-0
    1. Germany (West)—Foreign economic relations—Soviet
Union. 2. Soviet Union—Foreign economic relations—Germany
(West) 3. Christians, F. Wilhelm—Journeys—Soviet Union.
4. Soviet Union—Description and travel—1970–   I. Title.
HF 1546.15.S65C47 1990
337.43047—dc20   90-42165   CIP

Macmillan books are available at special discounts for bulk purchases
for sales promotions, premiums, fund-raising, or educational use. For
details, contact:
            Special Sales Director
         Macmillan Publishing Company
              866 Third Avenue
             New York, NY 10022

          10 9 8 7 6 5 4 3 2 1

          Printed and bound by
  Quebecor America Book Group, Brattleboro, VT

We Russians are a young nation; we are only just beginning to live although we have been in existence for a thousand years already; however, a large ship requires a long voyage.

DOSTOEVSKY

CONTENTS

FOREWORD

A top German banker writing about his experiences with the Russians and the Soviet system. How unusual! F. Wilhelm Christians is by no means a Sovietologist. Instead he is a successful businessman, albeit well educated in literature and in the history of the arts, modern and contemporary art in particular. And he is ever aware of his own experience as a very young lieutenant in Hitler's Wehrmacht invading the Soviet Union and fighting Stalin's Red Army.

This book ought to be read by those who over the last five decades have alternated between enthusiasm for "Uncle Joe" Stalin and abhorrence of the same man, between disgust over the "evil empire" and secret sympathy for Gorbachev, even if growing only slowly and hesitatingly. This book is easy to read; one may absorb it in just one evening. But it also offers good insight into the psyche of the Russians and into the nature and structure of the communist *nomenclatura* before Gorbachev, as well as his struggle against the Orwellian Soviet octopus.

When I read this book I felt a distinct sympathy for the views and also for the conclusions of the author, whom I have known for more than twenty-five years. He describes the same experiences during the war that I had, the same observations when visiting the Soviet Union for the first time a quarter of a century

after the armistice, the same encounters with that specific mix of
Russian attitudes vis-à-vis us Germans: suspicion at the same time
as admiration; awful memories as well as hope for mutual understanding; plus the hope and expectation for cooperation.

Our German feelings toward our great Russian neighbor are no
less complex. As a schoolboy in the 1920s I learned how Russia,
Austria, and Prussia as accomplices had jointly eradicated Poland
at the end of the eighteenth century; we were taught to feel sorry
for the Poles. We also learned of Napoleon's wars and of his
abortive attempt to conquer Moscow (after having already defeated the greater part of Europe) and thus the Russian Empire.
I was educated to feel gratitude toward Czar Alexander I, whose
troops liberated my hometown of Hamburg from brutal Napole-
onic occupation. We were taught to deplore the termination in
1890 of Bismarck's agreement of support with St. Petersburg by
Kaiser Wilhelm II and to abhor Wilhelm's arrogance. World War
I did not appear to us to have been caused by our German nation
alone but rather as having been brought about jointly by the
mistaken policies of almost all the European powers. And we were
taught to think of the 1919 peace treaty of Versailles as being
unjust to Germany. At school we heard little or nothing about
the Soviet Union, but we witnessed bloody fights in our streets
between Communists and Nazis, and we were told that Moscow
was backing the Communists. At the same time our teachers
made us read Tolstoy, Dostoevsky, Turgenev, even Gorki. And
we were also educated to love Tchaikovsky and Mussorgsky.

F. Wilhelm Christians was ten years old when the Nazis rose
to power in 1933 (I was his senior by four years). When we left
school we were drafted and became soldiers. Within the air force
and army the effort to indoctrinate us with Nazi ideology was
rather feeble in view of the character of the Berlin leadership (one
of my generals referred to them disdainfully only as "the brown
ones"). But we were nevertheless indirectly influenced by the
absence of any reliable information about what was really happening in the outside world. And because of how the "enemy"

or "Ivan" was described to us soldiers, we felt as uneasy vis-à-vis Russian civilians as we did vis-à-vis the brown-uniformed Nazi administrators to our rear. But we believed it was our duty to fight for our country. Only after the war could we start our university education. Only then would we begin to understand the mistakes, the faults, and the crimes for which we had been used.

Did this very late education—which was called "reeducation" by some Americans—lead to a total turnabout in regard to Russia? Did we, because of feelings of guilt, become Russophiles or even peaceniks? No, we did not. Was there any temptation to accept communist ideas or to advocate a German-Soviet alignment à la Rapallo?* The answers to any such questions were negative for Dr. Christians as well as for the overwhelming majority of Germans, including the 16 million living in the Soviet zone of occupation (later called the German Democratic Republic) who suffered under communist dictatorship and the so-called Real Existing Socialism. The answers had already been deemed categorically negative by the two outstanding political leaders who presided over the initial postwar era in Germany: Konrad Adenauer, the Christian conservative who became the first chancellor, and Kurt Schumacher, the leader of the Social Democratic Party.

When, under Gorbachev, the Soviet Union for the first time exercised respect for self-determination of the nations outside the Soviet Union, it became clear in Poland, Hungary, East Germany, and Czechoslovakia that nowhere did the people feel any attachment to communism or to "Big Brother" in Moscow. But still, all

---

* In April 1922 the first world economic conference of the twentieth century—albeit without United States participation—attempted to a large degree to exclude the Soviet and German delegations since conference members did not want to recognize the USSR nor settle the German reparation payments in an acceptable fashion. As a result, at the Italian resort of Rapallo, practically overnight and to the total surprise of the Western Allies, Moscow and Berlin concluded a treaty on the basis of mutual recognition. Its most important points: resumption of diplomatic recognition, renunciation of mutual demands arising from the war, and cooperation in various areas.

these nations need to remember that the Soviet Union is nearby, that it will remain the largest military power on the Eurasian continent whether Gorbachev fails or prevails, that Russia has pursued expansionist strategies for centuries and after the demise of Gorbachev a return to the expansionist strategy cannot be excluded. Prudent Polish leaders have known all this for a long time, and so have prudent German leaders, whether in the political realm or in industry and banking.

France is Germany's most important neighbor and its closest partner; Russia (or the Soviet Union) is by far Germany's biggest and most powerful neighbor. We therefore need the Western alliance and the American presence in Europe as a counterweight. We particularly need the inseparable integration of the unified Germany within the European community. But we also hope and strive and work for good and cooperative relations with our great Russian neighbor that is as close by as it has been during the last three centuries. This, in essence, has been the overall German strategy concerning the Soviet Union for a quarter of a century: to be firmly rooted in the West, to be jointly capable of deterring the Soviet Union and, if necessary, of defending against it, on the one hand, but on the other hand, to cooperate with it economically, politically, and culturally, thereby trying to influence the Soviet Union to adopt the behavior of a benign neighbor within (to use a favorite metaphor of Gorbachev) the "common European house."

Dr. Christians was working from this strategic platform even before it was formulated as policy in the latter half of the 1960s. As an executive of Deutsche Bank he anticipated *Ostpolitik**
before it became part of the German global strategy. But like those federal chancellors who prepared and pursued Ostpolitik and the Helsinki Process,** he never left any of his Soviet counterparts

---

* Ostpolitik, initiated under the chancellorship of Willy Brandt in 1969, was designed to improve German-Soviet relations "in small steps through change and rapprochement."

** A process of regular consultation among thirty-five nations that began with

in doubt about his unquestionably firm position in the Western camp. This is most clearly conveyed in this book, that is, by his reporting on the conversations with his Soviet counterparts about the "Double-track" decision of NATO in 1979 which, because of the massive deployment of Soviet SS-20 missiles, called for deploying 108 Pershing II and 464 cruise missiles; this led in the end to the zero-zero agreement on Intermediate Nuclear Forces we had sought from the beginning.

It was not easy to convince the Carter White House of the necessity to counterbalance the quickly growing, enormous SS-20 threat against Western Europe, although this effort, foreseeable enough, took a much greater political toll on the German, Dutch, Danish, Belgian, and Italian prime ministers than on the U.S. president. Conversely, the White House has always been very quick to demand that we participate in "letting the Soviets pay the price" or "punishing Moscow" by means of economic or trade warfare. The bitter dispute between the United States and us Europeans, France's President Mitterand and particularly me, over the European-Soviet pipeline deal is a striking example. Christians correctly describes our motivation (namely diversification of our imports of primary energy since we did not have considerable quantities of oil and gas in our own territory) and at the same time our self-imposed limitations on Soviet gas imports. In order not to become dependent on Soviet deliveries, my government had put a ceiling on Russian gas imports of no more than thirty percent of our natural gas consumption and, even more important, of no more than five percent of our total consumption of primary energy, our degree of dependence on OPEC deliveries still remaining many times higher. President Reagan obviously neither knew this nor bothered to listen to us.

Time and again American administrations have allowed them-

---

the 1975 Helsinki Conference on Security and Cooperation in Europe; a document was signed agreeing to basic human rights, nonintervention in internal affairs, and the renouncing of armed intervention or threats and acts of military, economic, and political coercion.

selves to be misled about the volume of our trade with the Soviet Union. At the end of my chancellorship, German exports to the Soviet Union amounted to less than two percent of our total exports, and our imports from the Soviet Union were minimal as well. The Soviet Union has almost forty times the population of Austria, but our trade with Vienna was three times as large as our trade with Moscow. These relations have barely changed over the decades. It often seemed as if American political advisers were unable to comprehend world trade statistics. Dr. Christians, along with me, has been a promoter of German-Russian trade; we were often obliged to stave off American criticism and even open intervention, of which this book gives a good overview.

We were (and still are) convinced that German-Russian trade was much more important for the Soviets than for us because they could offer us only oil and gas and other commodities while we had first-class machinery and other investment goods that they needed dearly. From the point of view of our strategic concept, it was (and still is) advantageous for us to keep the Soviets interested in maintaining good economic relations with Germany and, therefore, good relations in general.

It has frequently happened that somebody in Moscow tried to intimidate the German partner. This book reports how Christians, as the co-chairman of the Deutsche Bank's board of managing directors, stood up against such attempts in the same way I did as a federal chancellor. Like me, he also insisted on placing a wreath at the graves of German soldiers. And he walked out on a high-ranking Soviet official who became insulting. But Dr. Christians also met high-ranking Soviets who fought in the same battles in the "Great Patriotic War," and they exchanged experiences. Dr. Christians was motivated by his conviction that such a tragedy must never be permitted to happen again. He understands the Russians better than many other Westerners, their Dostoevskian messianism and their superiority complex as well as their inferiority complex.

His account of the Soviet economy is enlightening in some

striking details, such as that Premier Tikhonov under Brezhnev
in 1975 did not know the level of Soviet gold reserves; that
Gorbachev in 1989 did not know the money supply figures or
how many rubles were in circulation; that in 1983 under Andropov the Russians still had no fewer than eleven ministries
dealing with agriculture (I remember a special Ministry of Bread
and Bakery). Andropov, who died after serving just one year as
general secretary, was the first to try decentralization, which Dr.
Christians at the time called a "mental atomic bomb" because he
foresaw the enormous and unavoidable social and economic im-
plications of decentralization. Gorbachev's experiences half a
decade later have proved Dr. Christians right.

Dr. Christians has always declined subsidizing interest on credits to the Soviet Union, just as the Bonn government did, but he
pleads in favor of a helpful attitude on the part of the West
toward President Gorbachev. If his courageous endeavor of reform fails, it will be to the detriment of the Russians, all the other
nations and nationalities inside the Soviet Union, and her neighbors as well. But if Gorbachev succeeds, it will benefit everybody.
To achieve success will require enormous effort and prerequisites,
the least of which will be far-reaching agreements on arms reduction. But I agree with F. Wilhelm Christians: We have reason to
hope that out of the horrible and tragic experiences of our dreadful century there will emerge the concept, and the will, to make
the process of peaceful change irreversible.

HELMUT SCHMIDT
Former Chancellor of the
Federal Republic of Germany

ACKNOWLEDGMENTS

Special thanks to Mr. John O. Koehler for his editorial guidance and invaluable help in the production of this book. Mr. Koehler's knowledge of both the author and the subject, his personal candor, his immediate responses to all queries, and his tireless cooperation helped to make this book possible.

Thanks also to translator Joachim Neugroschel and to copy editors Carole McCurdy and Rose Ann Ferrick.

1 · RUSSIA AGAIN

The DC-9 of Austrian Airlines had been flying over Soviet territory for more than an hour already, having taken off from Vienna. In December 1969 any German who wanted to visit Moscow had to use Austrian Airlines. Germany's Lufthansa did not yet have landing rights in the Soviet capital. The hot war had ended only twenty-five years ago, and the cold war was still going strong.

Below me lay the vast snowy fields of the Ukraine. All you could make out of the white wasteland through the mist was the dark ribbon of the Dnieper River and the blurry outlines of Kiev. Then we soared over the gigantic forests of Konotop. Snow, snow, and more snow. It had been the same back then, during the Russian winters when Adolf Hitler had awarded us "Frozen Meat Medals"—campaign medals so-nicknamed because of the millions of frozen limbs suffered by German soldiers.

The Shisdra River must have been flowing somewhere down there. Once I had nearly remained on its banks forever. It had happened in 1942 during the second Russian winter. We were bivouacked in a huge forest; for weeks on end we had been fighting to defend it against Siberian machine gunners. My brother had fallen in action nearby, and early one morning I had gone looking for his grave. Later on I rode an armored reconnaissance car to a clearing in order to make contact with an artillery

1

observer we thought was stationed there. I was hit just as I was getting out of the vehicle. It was my third wound and my worst.

The bullet from the sniper perched in a tree had grazed the rim of my steel helmet, penetrated my shoulder, and lodged in my left lung. With blood pouring from my mouth and nose, I lay in the snow and waited for my comrades, expecting my enemy to deliver the coup de grace at any moment. It took a long time before help finally arrived.

Even today I have to chuckle at the way I misread my anatomy back then. In a semiconscious state as I was being examined by a medical orderly in a shack, I heard him clearly say, "The lieutenant received a clean shot in the left side of his chest." I was relieved to hear it. Since I thought the heart was in the "right place," I figured I would pull through once again.

Well, despite my anatomical confusion, I did survive, and now, in early December 1969, I was sitting in an airplane bound for Moscow as a representative of Deutsche Bank to negotiate a huge Soviet-German industrial project. The increase in cabin pressure signaled that we were about to land. The DC-9 made a wide loop. Below me, the Soviet capital's gigantic sea of houses came rushing up through the haze. Moscow: a mirage for millions of German soldiers who never reached it. The seat of the greatest military power on earth, the deadliest threat to the West—that was how it was described in those days.

Moscow-Sheremetyevo was the capital's civil airport. Its terminal was completely inadequate; it was not until 1980, the year of the Olympics, that Sheremetyevo II, a modern facility, was built in record time by a German firm, which modeled it after Hannover-Langenhagen Airport. As I walked down the gangway I was instantly engulfed in a cloud of an unmistakably Russian fragrance, a blend of many things: the fumes of Russia's low-octane gasoline; the pungent stench of ubiquitously used cheap laundry soap and disinfectants; and the smoke of the Makhorka *papyrossi*—hand-rolled cigarettes consisting of *Pravda* newsprint and finely chopped tobacco leaf stems, which the Red Army men had carried loosely in their pockets during World War II.

All at once it dawned on me: I was in a country that I had invaded twenty-five years earlier, following orders; and now, as the representative of a new and different Germany, I was supposed to establish the first postwar contacts with Soviet political and financial leaders.

All along the way I found the people polite but clearly aloof, revealing their natural Russian distrust of foreigners. I had to wait a long time for my passport and my baggage to be checked. Conversation was tentative. Then we began the long drive to the center of Moscow. On the wide access road from the northwest there is a monument marking the place where the spearhead of German tanks was finally halted forever in the late fall of 1941. Not far from the monument I spotted a poster adorning a wall; it showed a delicate flower blossoming in a furrow and the ominous shadow of a German army boot falling across it. The war, the Great Patriotic War, was and is by no means forgotten.

I had to stop saying "Russia" and get used to employing the official name of this country: the Union of Soviet Socialist Republics, USSR, or Soviet Union for short. And the people I would be dealing with were Soviets, not Russians, unless they were specifically ethnic Russians. The people I negotiated with placed great value on correct wording, especially in contracts.

I soon had an opportunity to reverse the situation with them, however. The Soviets liked to use the initials F. R. G. instead of Federal Republic of Germany. Citing our constitution, I always stipulated that our country's name be spelled out. My insistence led to a grotesque predicament when we finally signed the extensive loan agreement for the Yamal pipeline after years of negotiating (from 1979 to 1982). Just before the signing ceremony in Leningrad, a protocol ritual of great pomp and circumstance, I again noticed that ominous abbreviation F. R. G. in the text of the agreement. I asked the Soviets to correct it. Wringing their hands, they reminded me of the time pressure, the waiting television journalists, and our planned statements to the national and international press. But I insisted, and the change was made.

On my arrival in Moscow, during the final leg of our long drive to the center, we had a fantastic view of the gilded dome of the Kremlin. And then our car pulled up at the Hotel National, the deluxe and tradition-steeped building at the end of Gorky Prospekt, across from the walls of the Kremlin. Once again we had to wait at the reception desk until our papers and belongings were examined. But at last we were taken to our rooms.

The edifice, constructed under the czars, luxuriates in elements of art nouveau, which were being meticulously restored. Everything here breathes history, both aristocratic and revolutionary. German Communist refugees—Wehner, Leonhardt, and many others—stayed here during the thirties and forties; not all of them escaped Stalin's secret police. All these thoughts flashed through my mind as I strode on the thick carpets of the long corridors.

Not far from the Hotel National, the Metropol, with its similar atmosphere, stands opposite the Bolshoi Theater. It was at the Metropol that we spent many years in our first Moscow office for Deutsche Bank, together with other West German and West European firms. Built by a German businessman at the turn of the century, the Metropol had a presidential suite sumptuously decked out with gold and red velvet; it was off the same corridor as our office. From the side window of the suite you could glimpse—appropriately—the KGB headquarters in the background. Later on I often resided in the splendid rooms of the Metropol. To get to our office I merely had to step across the hall.

However, my accommodations were less comfortable during my first visit to Moscow in December 1969. Our room at the National was located in the dark rear wing of the hotel. When I opened the door, a tiny, frightened mouse scurried away. The furnishings were sparse, and the room looked hostile and repulsive. A naked light bulb on a long wire dangled from the ceiling, and the black windows faced an unlit inner courtyard. When I tried to improve the dreary image by drawing the curtain, the strings became tangled, and the whole contraption came crashing down. After that I refrained from any further efforts to make the place more livable. In Moscow you quickly develop a thick skin against such mishaps.

Still and all, my memories of the National are filled with nostalgia. During my more than thirty trips to the Soviet Union I got to stay there now and then. Soon I was "promoted" to the *bel étage.* On many evenings after a long day's work I would stand at the window, engrossed in the view of the enormous square: to the left, city hall; opposite me, the wide, steep approach to Red Square with Lenin's tomb and the gigantic G.U.M. department store, the imposing façade of the Kremlin, and the many spires of St. Basil's Cathedral; to the right, the former imperial stables, now used chiefly for art exhibitions; the broad green belt at the bottom of the sixty-foot Kremlin wall, with the Tomb of the Unknown Soldier and the eternal flame.

I have often stood on the balcony of the *bel étage* staring at that corner where newlyweds stepped into waiting taxis that had previously dropped them off at this entranceway to Red Square and Lenin's tomb. If you looked at their facial features, you could usually guess from which region of the gigantic realm they had traveled to the capital in order to join together for life. The walk to the mausoleum of the man who had founded the Soviet Union seemed like a solemn, almost religious ceremony: They would place the bridal nosegay or a bouquet of red carnations on the tomb and, posing in front of the tremendous cube, have their photo snapped for posterity.

That first night in Moscow in December 1969, I was unable to fall asleep in my shabby hotel room. Too many impressions and recollections kept me awake. I got dressed, squeezed past the unavoidable female supervisor stationed in the hallway to guard the keys, and went out into the street. It was an icy, crystal-clear winter night. On Red Square the hard snow, packed solid by thousands of feet, crunched under my shoes. What did it remind me of?

My eyes wandered over to the two motionless Red Army men flanking the entrance to Lenin's tomb; they seemed hewn out of marble. From there my eyes shifted to the Ministerial Council Building where the highest executive authority in the Soviet Union holds its meetings. On the dome a gigantic red banner was billowing lazily in the night wind; with spotlights sharply slicing it out of the blue darkness, the silk cloth emanated triumph, almost majesty. A few windows in the enormous edifice were still lit. Who, I wondered, could be poring over files in there? Who were these apparatchiks with absolute, unhampered power over 285 million human beings? And what about the men I would soon be facing; what were they like? In the nocturnal hush, the citadel, a cross between a monastery and a defiant fortress, the core of a terrifying empire, exuded a mysterious fascination.

Was I still a victim of prejudices that had shaped my image of Russia for decades? The big red stars on the pinnacles of the towers sent shivers through me. They evoked associations with things I had suppressed for such a long time. Those same stars had decorated the caps and belt buckles of the Red Army men we had confronted for months on end, and they had adorned the turrets of their tanks, which had chased us like rabbits when we retreated. Did we hate the Russian soldiers? And what had happened when our government had tried to instil in us an almost fanatical hatred of anything Soviet?

We had all been thunderstruck by the brutal swing of Hitler's policies. Barely two years after the signing of the so-called Friendship Treaty of August 1939, we were ordered to invade Russia. Overnight the Nazi propaganda machine had to create an image of the enemy that would spur us to attack. Out of the blue, the Soviet Union, which had been our friend just yesterday, became the epitome of absolute evil. Moscow was the heart of an uncontrolled and merciless foe who was about to stab a peace-loving Greater German Reich in the back. Horrifying pictures showed us the threat that the German soldier, indeed the entire German people, would be facing if we did not win this war. Stalin, painted as a hundred times worse than Ivan the Terrible, would then attack us with his "Jewish-Bolshevik commissars" and his "Asiatic hordes," who would kill and burn their way across the continent and bring all of Western Europe to its knees. The "Big Lie" was the order of the day.

Until just a few days before the invasion was launched on June 22, 1941, however, an entirely different story had been circulating through our army staging areas. According to both the scuttle-butt of the rank and file and the official communiqués to the officers, massive numbers of German troops had been deployed to Poland, and Moscow was allowing them to march peacefully through the southern part of the Soviet Union with the goal of defending the strategically vital Baku oilfields on the Black Sea against hostile—that is, British—assaults. But now German propaganda slickly pulled an about-face and confronted us with the warped image of a ruthless foe. All at once we were enmeshed in an ideological war as soldiers of a holy crusade. At stake was the very survival of Western civilization.

This idea of a crusade was adopted, like it or not, by our two division chaplains. In their Sunday sermons, which under the circumstances were rarely given, the pastors used the Maltese cross (which also decorated our tanks and other vehicles) to imbue us with the proper attitude in our "battle against the infidel." At the start of the assault the "Commissar Order" was issued, requiring the immediate execution of any and all *polit-ruks*—Red Army political officers—who fell into our hands. But our unit refused to obey this command. The fact that it was issued was not surprising, however, given the well-nigh hysterical propaganda that accompanied us as we marched against the Soviet Union.

Not only was the enemy depicted as satanic, but we were exhorted not to fall into his hands no matter the circumstances. German soldiers, and especially officers, could, we were told, expect no mercy. And the commissars in particular would give no quarter. In hindsight I must admit that such warnings had their desired effect. German soldiers actually heaved a sigh of relief if they were wounded or transferred to a different sector because that meant escaping the witches' cauldron of Russia. Until the bitter end, the German soldier identified his Russian adversary with a cruel and merciless regime.

But this image did not apply to the Russians as people. After all, we had more than enough opportunity to get to know them during long winter months of static warfare. In the summer of 1941 we were dumbstruck when portions of the Ukrainian population welcomed us with garlands and the traditional presents for visitors. German propaganda quickly came up with an explanation: The miserable Russian people had been waiting for the Wehrmacht to liberate them from the Stalinist terror. This wave of friendliness lasted for a while, then the climate changed at one stroke when we were followed by SD (Security Service) units, which created "order" in their own way. In regard to the real or alleged cruelty of this war, we were at least on a par with the other side.

My mind was teeming with all these memories the night of my first return to Russia. With my coat collar turned up and my hands buried deep in my pockets, I gazed at the illuminated windows of the Kremlin. A long time later I myself stood behind those windows, staring down at the people in Red Square. By then I was an honored guest of the men who, on that December night, were still faceless for me—rigid functionaries of a cold power machine, the men we saw on the politburo grandstand at the parades celebrating the October revolution.

During my first visit to Moscow and for years afterward, I kept rediscovering how devotedly the Soviets kept alive the memory of what they call the Great Patriotic War and how deeply menaced they felt by the possibility of a new war. By now the West Germans had come to terms with their own situation: Benefiting from a thriving economy, they were busy transforming a portion of a divided Germany into a free, self-sufficient country in which life was worth living. Yet whenever I negotiated with the Soviets, I could always sense nervousness about a threat of war. In the West, people have often wondered how the powerful Soviet Union could possibly fall prey to this trauma. To a German living in the small Federal Republic, with its limited military power, the Soviet fear is puzzling. I tried to fathom it during numerous talks with the Soviets.

What did I learn in the process? Geographically, the Soviet Union is the largest country in the world. A distance of some six thousand miles separates Brest Litovsk in the west from Vladivostok in the east. If we include Sakhalin Island, which is Soviet territory, the distance amounts to seventy-two hundred miles end to end. The distance from north to south is twenty-five hundred to thirty-five hundred miles. The European part of the Soviet Union, which we generally identify with Russia, has virtually no natural defenses protecting its borders. Does anyone realize that the tallest point within this gigantic realm is to be found in the Valday Hills, which are not even fourteen hundred feet above sea level? Throughout history this empire, partly because of its topographic configuration, has always been exposed and vulnerable to any attack from west or east. Tartars and Mongols invaded it, occupying the land and mistreating the inhabitants for centuries. And so did Western armies. In 1812, Napoleon marched into Moscow. During World War I, German troops pushed almost all the way to Minsk. Such experiences cannot fail to leave an impression on a nation's mind.

Perhaps I became aware of all these things only later on, in the course of my travels and not during that lonesome evening on Red Square when I was still suffering from the shock of my first encounter with the Soviet superpower. It was not until later that I began to try to understand this country's security problems or, rather, traumas by seeing them from the Soviet point of view and thereby trying to fathom some of their erratic reactions. This approach became my guideline throughout my later contacts with these people.

The day after my arrival I went to the Foreign Trade Bank to start our negotiations, which was why I had come to the Soviet Union.

2 · A MISSION TO MOSCOW: NEGOTIATIONS

How did this trip originate? During the 1969 Hannover Industrial Fair, Nikolai S. Patolichev, then Soviet minister of foreign trade and a veteran of the Russian revolution, opened the door to the West—just a crack. Explaining the policy of his country, he said that the Soviet Union would be "receptive" to imports of Western machinery and capital goods. Apparently it had dawned on the Soviets that the boasts made by Nikita S. Khrushchev after his 1959 trip to the United States would not materialize for a long time if at all. The Soviet leader had declared that it was only a matter of years before the USSR caught up with America's industrial development and standard of living. *Dognat i peregnat*, "to catch up and overtake," was Khrushchev's favorite saying in those days. Patolichev now announced that the Soviets wanted to begin explicit negotiations about cooperating with the West and importing Western "machinery plants."

The first major German firm to be approached was Mannesmann; they were asked to provide large-diameter steel pipes for natural gas lines. Mannesmann had experience in doing business in Russia. Back in 1890, the year it was founded, this Düsseldorf firm, in close collaboration with Deutsche Bank, had provided the first seamless steel line for a Russian factory (in the Caucasus). Then, at the turn of the century, it built the renowned 540-mile oil pipeline from Baku to Batum on the Black Sea. As of 1912, Mannesmann was known as the "royal supplier" of oil pipes to the czars. After the October Revolution (in 1917), relations with the East European trading partner were quick to revive. And by 1926, Deutsche Bank assumed leadership of a large German banking syndicate that had been set up to underwrite German exports to the USSR.

Now, in 1969, the question of long-term financing arose once again. Since I was on the supervisory board of Mannesmann Pipes, this issue became my responsibility within Deutsche Bank's board of directors. From the very start I conducted the negotiations with keen interest and commitment. In fact, for some time now I had been studying the history of German-Russian relations. Coincidentally, in 1969 we were getting ready for Deutsche Bank's centennial celebration in April 1970. We had hired a knowledgeable writer to chronicle the outstanding events in the history of our bank, including, of course, the above-described task of financing German-Russian trade. Thus, a certain tradition already existed, and we expanded on it with a number of ideas.

Furthermore, there were the events of the 1950s and '60s with the ebb and flow of the Cold War. I was convinced that the separation and severing of ties caused by the building of the Berlin wall could not be permanent. To my mind, the resumption of at least reasonable economic relations through cautious contacts was merely a question of time.

In 1962, under American pressure, the West German government declared the so-called pipe embargo: No equipment for building pipelines could be exported to the USSR. This setback, a bitter disappointment, had serious consequences. The often observed distrust of the Soviets toward their Western partners now waxed even stronger. And on the German side, the embargo led to a certain alienation from and finally aloofness toward Moscow. We grew further and further apart—for seven years.

Listening to the hints of Foreign Trade Minister Patolichev

about the possibilities of exporting to the Soviet Union, I now sensed a chance for a new beginning. And in my optimism I felt that this would also pave the way for an eventual easing of political tensions.

In the spring of 1969, right after Patolichev's comments in Hannover, I received a visitor at my Düsseldorf office: Mevodiy Naumovich Sveshnikov, chairman of the Soviet Foreign Trade Bank. He wanted to talk to me about a loan of billions of marks to fund the importing of Mannesmann large-diameter pipes for the construction of a gas pipeline. He was the first Soviet I negotiated with, and our business deal was to be my first of this kind. Its basic pattern was later followed again and again: The Germans would supply the pipes in exchange for Soviet natural gas, and the entire transaction would be underwritten by a German banking syndicate. The loan would be repaid in the form of subsequent deliveries of gas. In other words, this was a simple and lucid three-sided deal; it could be handled in a reasonable way, and its purpose was clearly defined.

After Mr. Sveshnikov's visit to Düsseldorf, I reciprocated by taking my first trip to Moscow in order to continue negotiating our agreement. From preliminary talks with my colleagues during our flight and later at the hotel, we were fully aware that our job would not be easy. Our minds were reeling from the stories we had heard from businessmen of wild things that happened when they had previously visited Moscow. The Soviets, we were told, did not hesitate to employ seductive young women to chat with us in the evening and ferret out our goals and terms. Naturally, we took it for granted that our hotel rooms would be bugged. All of us seriously reckoned with the use of such "intelligence" methods by our hosts, for we considered ourselves and the object of our talks important enough to merit "special attention."

We had even gotten some advice on how to minimize the risk of being overheard in rooms that were presumably bugged: Sit down on the edge of the bathtub and turn on the water full blast. The resulting gush would be so noisy that no eavesdropper could possibly pick up our bathroom conversation. I also made frequent use of an offer from Moscow's German embassy: Whenever I had to have sensitive telephone conversations with people in West Germany, I could use the embassy's Faraday cage, an absolutely bug-proof booth.

Our first negotiations took place at the Foreign Trade Bank, which has since been renamed the Bank for Foreign Economic Affairs. In those days it was located near the splendid edifice of Gosbank, the national bank of the Soviet Union. Until the restructuring of the Soviet banking system in 1988, this central bank, with its more than eighty thousand branches, was responsible for every domestic banking transaction within the Soviet Union. To some extent—as I soon noticed in my negotiations—it also dominated the Foreign Trade Bank, which was in charge of dealing with foreign commercial banks. At times I even sensed a rivalry between the two institutions. The head of Gosbank is also a member of the cabinet, which gives him political clout. For many years this position was filled by Vladimir S. Alkhimov, about whom I will have more to say later. We had a good rapport, based on our professional backgrounds, which helped us overcome several obstacles. This was especially true in the often critical Yamal pipeline talks that lasted from 1979 to 1982.

During the twenty years of my negotiations, the Foreign Trade Bank relocated several times. Its offices were always very unassuming. I must express my admiration for this bank: Even though its business volume kept expanding year after year, its employees always managed to get a job done on time despite external difficulties. Many years ago I was shown the impressive model of a new building that was to house all the financial institutions based in Moscow. In late 1989 they were finally able to occupy this gigantic high-rise.

When we began our loan talks in 1969, a certain physical pattern quickly emerged; since it proved quite workable, we kept it to the end. I usually arrived with two associates who sat to my left and my right, while the Soviet delegation, consisting of five to ten members and sometimes even more, settled on the other side of the table. I soon got to understand which language would be best suited for such proceedings and which overall strategy would be most serviceable. I later exchanged my insights with people at the West German Foreign Office in Bonn.

I would like to mention my capable associates from the bank who throughout the years of negotiations efficiently backed me up with the necessary stamina, patience, and tenacity. There are two in particular whom I would like to name: Dr. Ernst Taubner, head of trade finance, who was already well experienced in dealing with the Soviet Union; he accompanied me from the outset. Dr. Axel Lebahn joined us in 1979; not only did he have perfect command of the Russian language, but also, having studied at Moscow University, he was familiar with the country and its people.

At our very first meeting the Soviet side made it clear that formal negotiations were always to be conducted in both German and Russian; but naturally, on informal occasions and during breaks or meals, we could converse in other languages, say, English or French. In the course of my visits I noticed that languages were a strong point in the educational background of the Soviet team. English had a distinct lead over German. I admired the proficiency of our Soviet interpreters, who spoke German with no trace of an accent. I also realized—and this was confirmed by the West German Foreign Office—that it makes a lot of sense to handle concrete negotiations in one's native tongue. This produced a give-and-take rhythm that, like a metronome, ticked off the dialogue in very precise terms.

As time went on I acquired a small Russian vocabulary, and I understood enough of the language to make out at least the most important words used by a Soviet negotiator, and I could more or less comprehend his meaning. Since I took pains to articulate slowly and clearly, the Russians followed suit. This approach, which was highly advantageous for all practical applications, was a good recipe to follow; the dialogue became more disciplined, the substance more concrete, and our goals were achieved in a more efficient manner.

My associates soon made me aware of something rather baffling: At nearly every session a KGB man was among the long row of Soviet negotiators. As a meeting got under way, my colleagues had time to size up the Soviets while I usually had to focus on whoever was heading their team. Eventually we developed a certain knack for identifying the KGB man rather quickly. During our later trips to the interior of the Soviet Union, we kept bumping into such travel companions. I got so used to them that soon I was no longer offended by their presence, nor did it ever keep me from expressing my opinion when it came time to criticize certain conditions.

The presumed representative of the secret service never took the floor. He merely listened and looked. The KGB, we were told, was ubiquitous; it was considered the best-informed Soviet institution, more so than the government or even the politburo. This KGB omnipresence made it difficult to meet privately with our counterparts in one-on-one negotiations. If we tried, we distinctly sensed the reluctance of the Soviets. I very seldom managed to invite a Soviet colleague to a private meeting; for instance, when Soviet delegations were visiting the Federal Republic, nobody dared to go solo, everyone had to feel observed in order to behave properly. "Big Brother is watching you."

Our three secretaries—Soviet citizens, of course—had been cleared by the KGB and were obliged to make regular reports. But this certainly did not mean that they were not efficient and personally reliable.

When my wife and I visited Tiflis in Soviet Georgia and Erivan in Armenia, I was able to have lengthy conversations with the local church leaders—but within earshot of an observer from the Ministry of the Interior. Both these Soviet republics are known as religious strongholds. The two patriarchs of the Orthodox Church went into great detail about church life in their parishes. I was deeply impressed by the patriarch of Armenia. In perfect

Oxford English he told me about the history of his people. Armenia, the land bridge between Europe and Asia, has been invaded, occupied, and looted repeatedly; and the Armenians, he said, have suffered all kinds of atrocities, including genocide. While speaking, this prince of the church motioned toward the imposing memorial on a hill looming over the city: With its eternal flame, this monument reminds travelers of those horrible times. The patriarch added that Armenia has been a Soviet republic for sixty years now and—by historical standards—this was the first period in which his nation could live in peace and quiet, and sleep without fear at night. But since our conversation it has become obvious how deceptive that peacefulness was. The age-old ethnic and cultural conflicts have erupted again.

Toward the end of 1969 I was in Moscow immersed in negotiating the huge triangular deal involving the exchange of credits and pipes for gas. In essence the Soviets needed money for developing their immense natural gas deposits in Siberia and exporting gas to the West. Now the specifics would have to be discussed.

Our talks advanced rather swiftly. On February 1, 1970, the formal signing of the agreement took place at the Kaiserhof in Essen. The participants in the ceremony included Foreign Trade Minister Patolichev on behalf of the Soviet government and Professor Karl Schiller, minister of economics, on behalf of the West German government. Their presence was to attest to the eminent political importance that this first major agreement had for *both* governments. However, it was not the ministers who did the signing. The German signatories were the representatives of the bank that had handled the loan negotiations, the chairman of Mannesman, as supplier of the pipes, and the chairman of Ruhrgas, as importer of the gas.

The Soviets always had a difficult time assessing the negotiation scene as well as my personal position. In Moscow I operated as the representative of my bank, Deutsche Bank, and also as the head of a German banking syndicate. The syndicate had issued a negotiating mandate for the chief negotiator. My bank, however, was a private institution and I, needless to say, was a private individual. And the syndicate itself was made up of private institutions—namely, a large group of German banks.

On the other hand, the Soviet negotiators were ministers, deputy ministers, heads of agencies in the various ministries, and so forth. They were led by a man whom I held in great esteem: Vladimir Alkhimov, the abovementioned president of the Soviet central bank (Gosbank). The Soviets also had constant problems with the fact that a relatively young man was coming to Moscow with extraordinary negotiating powers to talk with the Soviet government about credits amounting to billions. Even in their other contacts with Western countries, the Soviets were not used to dealing with private individuals exercising such mandates without the presence of a government representative. For years I tried to explain these matters to the Soviets and make the differences between our systems clear regarding my own field as well, but ultimately, I fear, my efforts were in vain. Their imagination was too remote from ours. It was molded by the all-encompassing jurisdiction of the state.

Furthermore, we Germans differed in many respects from other Western negotiating teams. In contrast to nearly all Western countries, Bonn did not grant interest subsidies. Moscow often urged us to reduce our interest rates by drawing on West German government funds. This issue was debated in Bonn, and not all voices were negative. But I urgently advised against giving in; I feared that once the precedent was established there would be no way of stemming the demands of our Moscow partners. I was also worried that it might greatly undermine the expense structure and the discipline of our negotiations. Representatives of other COMECON* countries had approached me with similar requests. A Polish representative had even said that "Big Brother" in Moscow received too many concessions as it was. If we had backed down on the issue of interest subsidies during the early 1970s, the

* The Council for Mutual Economic Assistance (COMECON) is the Eastern Bloc's answer to the European Economic Community (EEC).

results of this precedent, as can be easily calculated, would have been highly disadvantageous to our side. Other Western negotiators offered the Soviets government-subsidized interest rates as a matter of course; but despite our handicap in dealing with the Soviet Union, West German industry managed to conclude extensive agreements during the 1970s and 1980s.

Incidentally, if the interest rates had been subsidized by Bonn, then our government—that is, the Ministry of Economics, the Ministry of Finances, the Foreign Office, or the central bank— would certainly have, if not negotiated directly, at least sent representatives to the proceedings. This, I repeat, was never the case on our side, either during the initial rounds in 1969–70 or later on. But needless to say, I kept Bonn posted on my impressions and the results of our work.

At times I got into certain predicaments because of misjudgments on the Soviet side. Let me offer one example, which can be understood only against the historical background. On August 12, 1970, the so-called Moscow Agreement was signed by Willy Brandt, the West German chancellor, and Leonid Brezhnev, the chief of the Soviet Communist Party. By its very nature this agreement also had an effect on commercial negotiations. In all my loan talks with the Soviets, their greatest bête noire had always been the clause regarding interest rates, which was not surprising given the huge sums that were at stake. On this score it was always particularly difficult to allay the distrust regarding my position on the interest rates especially because the Soviets generally believed that capitalists—and they considered me to be an unadulterated representative of this dubious species—wanted nothing better than to hoodwink a decent, idealistic Communist.

In this connection a minor incident occurred in the late sixties during our first round of talks. Accompanied by an official of the West German embassy, I was paying visits to various high-ranking functionaries. As a representative of "plutocracy" I had braced myself for queasy and standoffish reactions, perhaps even repugnance. In the eyes of these people I was the personification of anti-ideology, the embodiment of the capitalist class enemy. As I shook hands with them when saying good-bye, the embassy official whispered to me that some of these gentlemen would now probably hurry off to wash their right hands. I was amused, for I had been invited to Moscow after the conclusion of negotiations to put the finishing touches to the transactions that the Soviets wanted. Throughout our continual and extensive dealings during the following years, I often thought about that incident. It seemed to me that those long years of frequent meetings led to personal contact, and my opposite numbers might have detected some human features in this "profit-hungry capitalist." On the other hand, I wondered if such a discovery might have damaged my authority as chief negotiator.

In 1972 when I once again faced a large Soviet delegation (this time at the Soviet Foreign Trade Ministry), its leader, Mr. Patolichev's deputy, Nikolai D. Komarov, kept nagging me to sharply lower the interest rate. We haggled until I ran out of arguments. Mr. Komarov kept repeating: "Dr. Christians, you have to give in. Otherwise you'll be violating the agreement between our general secretary and your chancellor. I'll have no choice but to inform Herrn Brandt of your obstinacy."

Unfazed, I cordially replied: "Mr. Komarov, naturally I respect that agreement. But we are negotiating something that is outside the jurisdiction of my government. I am not a representative of my government, and I am therefore not subject to any instructions from the federal chancellor. I have to use my own judgment, and I have already clearly explained my position to you several times."

He nevertheless kept pounding away at me, and so I finally said: "Mr. Komarov, I'm sorry, I can do nothing but continue making the some offer and, if need be, rephrasing it. I cannot back down any further. We have a saying in Germany: 'Only a rascal promises more than he can deliver.' "

No sooner had I finished than Mr. Komarov leaped up, glaring and snapping: "Fine, Christians, you've told me a story. It was brief. And now I'm going to tell you a story, too, but mine is a little longer." He then recited a story concerning a czarist tax collector who came to Tiflis in order to question a businessman about his tax debt. The businessman's answers were long-winded and evasive, so the tax collector cut in and said: "If you can't tell me anything more, if all you can do is stall and tell me stupid things, then shut up!"

When I heard that, my patience snapped. I stood up, walked around the table, and headed toward the door. Komarov gaped at me. After all, this man was deputy minister of foreign trade, and he was flanked by high-ranking representatives of ministries and banks. When I was outside, he came after me and shook my hand. Then I wordlessly left the ministry. As serious as the goal of our talks may have been, the scene was not without its comical side.

Some two hours later, around noon, I was at my hotel, Intourist, when I received a message from the Kremlin. It came from Deputy Premier Vladimir N. Novikov, who was in charge of negotiations with West Germany. An extremely likable and realistic man, he was also a fair and capable negotiator. In his message he asked whether I would care to visit him at the Kremlin that afternoon. His car would pick me up at my hotel. I agreed, and that was how I first penetrated the vast inner sanctum of the Soviet Union. The drive took me past many interesting sights, including wonderful churches and the cracked bell from the days of Ivan the Great. Finally, we reached the government district, which was guarded by soldiers clutching Kalashnikov automatic rifles.

I entered Mr. Novikov's office. The deputy premier stood there waiting for me. He was a giant of a man, but his face was kind and open. Shaking my hand, he practically pulled me toward him like a father and spoke soothingly: "Okay, Christians, now we're going to sit down and talk calmly, the way we Soviet citizens talk, about the relations between our two countries."

Our conversation was intense, and it went on for quite a while. This was a seminal experience for me because it contained exactly what I had been after for a long time, at least in concept. Mr. Novikov and I strove to formulate a mutually useful analysis of the possibilities of cooperation between the enormous Soviet Union with its wealth of natural resources and the small but highly industrialized Federal Republic of Germany. I felt that the Soviet Union could export raw materials and semi-finished goods to West Germany in exchange for products and industrial processes that the Soviets needed to tap their vast natural resources. As it turned out, the two of us agreed on most issues, and we both envisioned vast possibilities of cooperation. But in practice it was a very long time before our two countries actually tried to use the existing opportunities. Even today, after seventeen years, we are still at the outset.

And so my day, which had begun so unpleasantly, ended on a conciliatory note, thanks to Mr. Novikov's bold concepts and personal charm. The deputy premier knew how to strike the right tone in order to gain a person's trust at the very start of a conversation. This bolstered his fine reputation not only with me but with many other German negotiators. Mr. Novikov proved that an individual *can* make a difference even in such a rigid, inflexible system.

3 · THE FIRST HINTS OF A
NEW WAY OF THINKING

The first major Soviet-German business deal, which was concluded in the winter of 1969–70, was followed by others within just a few years. In 1975 the Magirus company agreed to send trucks with air-cooled engines to the Soviet Union. This huge transaction was likewise financed by Deutsche Bank. The trucks were needed for building the famous Amur-Baikal-Magistrale railroad line; running at a length of eight hundred miles and parallel to the Trans-Siberian line, it was supposed to help the Soviets exploit their natural resources in Siberia—but its purposes were no doubt partly strategic. The railroad construction was plagued by horrible weather; and so the German Magirus trucks, which were well known in the Soviet Union for being robust and reliable, were ideal for the job.

Naturally, our dealings with Moscow, which did not and were never meant to remain secret, aroused skepticism, distrust, and perhaps even a little envy among our Western friends. Indeed, the United States government voiced some pointedly adverse criticism, which I will discuss in greater detail below. Even sharper reactions were provoked by the so-called Yamal pipeline agreement, which was negotiated between 1979 and 1982 with the participation of several Western European nations. The United States, with Secretary of State Alexander Haig in the lead, took a harsh stance against this multilateral contract. Major American newspapers accompanied our dialogue with frequently unfriendly comments. The main reproach was that by importing Soviet gas as their primary energy source, the Federal Republic of Germany and other Western countries would become overly dependent on the Soviet Union and therefore vulnerable to its political pressure during periods of tension. Moreover, the payments in hard Western currency would fill up the Soviet war chests.

The West German government, and also a portion of the German people, were not entirely immune to such reproaches. After all, we had learned a thing or two about energy dependence during the oil crunches of 1973 and 1978. After 1978, West Germany's position on fuel strategy basically called for two ways of reducing the priority of imports from the Arab Gulf states: Germany would diversify its primary fuel sources by using more coal and gas, and it would purchase energy from other non-OPEC countries. Our government, under Chancellor Helmut Schmidt, came to an informal agreement with the German industries that were involved: the gas user, the pipe manufacturer, and the financing banks. Gas imports from the Soviet Union were not to exceed five percent of the overall West German demand for primary energy, or thirty percent of the overall demand for natural gas. The upper limit was to be reached by the late 1980s. And indeed the situation developed as planned.

Despite these carefully calculated import parameters, which were based on rational government planning, the critical voices from the United States greatly interfered with our negotiations of the Yamal pipeline contract. Nor were the Americans alone in their skepticism. Their qualms were shared by numerous politicians in Bonn and representatives of the West German business world. My bank, as leader of the syndicate, was viewed more and more critically, and so was I. One or two banks even withdrew from the syndicate. What astonished me most was that while my dealings were greatly berated in public, I was asked in private whether I could make use of my allegedly good connections with Moscow to set up a visit to the Soviet capital by one or another high-ranking politician. And I also noted that certain banks which had left our syndicate because of the controversy decided to get back in on the action once the dark clouds had passed.

Those tensions put a terrible strain on the general climate, as can be seen in an incident typical of that period. In the Soviet government, Leonid Kostandov, by succeeding Deputy Premier Novikov, took over his job of supervising relations with the Federal Republic of Germany. A trained chemist, Kostandov had once worked in the Soviet chemical industry, and for that reason alone he advocated German-Soviet cooperation in the chemical industry and in the energy business with coal, gas, and oil. In June 1982, Kostandov visited West Germany for negotiations and also for talks in Bonn. Several appointments were set up for him, including one with me. When I went to see him, he looked somewhat depressed—much to my surprise, for he was by nature an open, enthusiastic, and extremely friendly man. I promptly learned the reason for his bad mood: In Bonn, Konstandov told me, people had turned a deaf ear to him. In fact, doors that had once been open to him were now being slammed in his face. The only explanation he could discern was the harsh American criticism. Perhaps, he said, it was partly due to the economic summit meeting that was just taking place in Paris; its agenda included the issue of energy supplies. Konstandov had the impression that the Bonn officials were scrambling to get to President Mitterand's gala reception at the palace of Versailles and therefore had neither the time nor the interest to see him. He was visibly happy that I was available. But then, I had not been invited to Versailles.

In my capacity as a private, purely commercial negotiator, I was again involved in the complicated political arena of East-West tensions. The Soviets expected me to take positions on issues that were not directly connected to my job. Their assumptions are easy to explain. After years of almost uninterrupted contact, my opposite numbers had become accustomed to my presence during my Moscow visits as well as their Western junkets, which grew more and more popular with them because of all the agreeable perks. Little by little we had developed a bond of trust.

But this was by no means the case at the outset. In the late sixties both sides were still very uneasy. One could often sense hostility among the Soviets. By the seventies, however, the group—obligated by the business at hand to get along with one another—had learned how to relax together despite residual skepticism. The rigidity of the early years had loosened, we knew one another, and at times we also thought highly of one another on a personal level. On the other hand, the Soviets could conveniently confront me with political questions—more often than I liked. Nor did they hold back with suspicions and even accusations. The Soviets may have found it feasible to treat me as a representative of German politics and enmesh me in problems about which I could not and would not make official political statements. They would often use me as a scapegoat when they wanted to vent their anger at the West Germans. After all, I was generally available.

In the spring of 1973 I reported this to Bonn, and when meeting with various government ministers, I discussed the philosophy I had worked out for conducting myself on the difficult Moscow terrain. I felt—and still feel—that the Soviets should be told that West Germany was not willing to sit on the sidelines, as it were. On the contrary: The Federal Republic was to be seen as a partner in the Western Alliance; its basic political position would not change, and its basic policies were not open to influence. The bottom line was that West Germany is and will remain a dependable member of NATO and the European Common Market.

I told our government that this should be made clear to the Soviets by the appropriate political agencies and not by me, for I was not authorized to do so. Once the Kremlin accepted this as an irrefutable fact, all of us, I said, would have a solid, mutually secure basis for extensive commercial agreements and also for much broader cooperation. I also asked the West German government to reach a decision on the irksome question of interest subsidies, which I was being obstinately pestered with. The verdict in Bonn, as I have already explained, was clearly negative. As far as I could determine there was no consensus in the cabinet, although the people who shaped the economic and financial policies obviously leaned toward my position.

A further problem had to be dealt with in regard to mutual understanding. It resulted from the fundamental gap between our political systems: On the one side, a liberal economy marked largely by private initiative, and on the other side, a stringently regulated central planning system. The Soviet delegates were acting on behalf of government authorities. They had to consider the goals of the current five-year plan as well as their own limited mandates.

We quickly realized that we had to study the Soviet system more closely in order to read the Soviet negotiators correctly— that is, understand their constant irritating reactions and their way of thinking. And so we familiarized ourselves with the methods and mentality of the Five-Year Plan.

In the Soviet Union "achievement"—and I use the term advisedly—is demonstrated chiefly by the attainment of a goal set by the central planners, for whom quality is a side issue. Since products are generally distributed by way of allocation, an occasional complaint may be voiced, but there is no mechanism for consumer feedback concerning the quality of products. The only "achievement" that counts for the individual worker is achieving the quota or, rather, recording this achievement in the appropriate documents. The quota is what rules the thoughts and actions of everyone involved in the production process, all the way up to the boss. The most important thing is not to make waves. Needless to say, this requires a lot of mutual back scratching. From there the path leads straight to corruption.

Not only has Mikhail Gorbachev recognized this predicament, but he has also addressed it forthrightly. He argues that if the Soviet economy is to meet the standards of the world economy, it must plan in terms of longer periods—at least ten years. Furthermore, he also demands quality along with quantity.

To implement this change, resistance must be overcome and disagreeable methods must be prescribed. The people charged with attaining the goals of the Five-Year Plan have developed an approach that is dramatically opposed to any concern for quality. Their minds focus purely on nominal, and therefore demonstrable, success, which they achieve "vertically" rather than "horizontally" by tailoring the processes to their personal areas of jurisdiction. Every department head, even on a ministry level, thinks only in terms of his own turf—and such egotism is actually rewarded. The outcome is a kind of tunnel vision. The individual stares through the narrow tunnel of his own area and sees only the quota figure. Heedless of whatever is happening to his right or left, he is never involved "horizontally," say, in the activities of neighboring agencies or ministries.

This attitude, which has been cultivated for decades, is bolstered by the teeming profusion of branch ministries. I have never managed to find out their exact number or their specific functions. Since this economic system is centrally ruled, it requires a central government agency for overall decision-making and coordination. And this is where the system is ridden into the ground. Endless armies of ministers and deputy ministers maintain an exorbitantly expensive apparatus in which each person cares only about his own turf. As a matter of principle, no allowances are made for appropriate and flexible adjustments and decisions on a local level anywhere in this enormous country. The result is gigantic inefficiency, and its sole beneficiaries are the more than 17 million functionaries who have every reason to defend their sinecures, which carry life tenure. Most of these officials were appointed during the Brezhnev era, which means they are middle-aged and still a long way from retirement. There seems to be no way of eliminating this huge encumbrance without causing a mass of turmoil.

In all fairness I have to admit that we, too, are threatened with vertical thinking and tunnel vision, both in government and in the centralized administration of huge firms—although with no-where near the magnitude of the Soviet authorities. We have repeatedly observed that despite the centralized and supposedly unified production planning, interaction is scarce in the Soviet Union. This alone makes coordination impossible, so that the effort and energy needed for the goal are never jointly determined and deployed. Various lines of implementation run side by side, often unconnected or even interfering with one another rather than promoting the overall efficiency. The upshot is that every-one seems to be running in place.

We had to experience this Soviet state of affairs for ourselves. As a result, when dealing with West Germany, ministries and lower-level institutions in Moscow would reach agreements that had not been previously cleared "horizontally" on the Soviet side. We usually knew what was involved in an individual case and the others with whom we had to deal, but coordination simply did not always materialize within the Soviet administra-tion. And this led to all kinds of unexpected difficulties or reser-vations. Now and then we would have to lend a hand by reaching through the red tape. In this way we unobtrusively contributed to achieving a common goal.

It all sounds very complicated, but it was a pragmatic way of overcoming an impasse. Meanwhile, things have started changing in the Soviet Union. Attempts are being made to reform the centralized planning, execution, and allocation of national re-sources. Reformers want to decentralize and redistribute author-ity, but Soviet minds are still too unaccustomed to this new way of thinking and attitudes are slow to change. Not only is this new approach unfamiliar, but it also puts a tremendous burden on the people operating within the traditional system. They now have to use their own judgment when making decisions, and occasion-ally they even have to deviate from the formulated plan. Earlier, such steps were utterly inconceivable. In fact, individuals think-ing and acting on their own would almost certainly have been accused of sabotage and duly punished rather than praised and duly rewarded with a promotion.

During the past few decades, however, the plan system has often been criticized even within the Soviet Union. Under Khrushchev and Kosygin, people often asked if efficiency could be improved by delegating responsibility and authority. Finally, during the 1980s, Yuri Andropov began to make efforts along those lines.

In 1982, after Brezhnev's death, Andropov became general secretary of the Soviet Communist Party. I vividly remember that a fresh new wind blew through the Moscow administration when he took office. Previously we had always felt as if we were dealing with occupants of stuffy, badly ventilated rooms who dozed their lives away, gloomy and phlegmatic, never mustering any initiative or joy in their work. But all at once the windows were flung wide open, and the change in attitude was almost palpable. These people came to life, their minds were more receptive, and they suddenly had the courage to view conditions critically and seek ways of improving them.

We noticed the first signs of this fresh breeze in the spring of 1983 when we were scheduled to meet with leaders of Gosplan, the influential architects of the centralized economic planning system. Once again we heard a variation on the theme of "decentralization of responsibility." This time, it seems, the initiative came directly from General Secretary Andropov. He had presented a study, done by a think tank in Novosibirsk, that had all the earmarks of a scientific approach. Scientific, mind you, which meant that the study could not be instantly pigeonholed as political. Afterward we wondered if Andropov had sent up a trial balloon.

During this meeting I asked N. N. Inosemtsev, deputy chief of Gosplan, what this study meant. He assured me, in front of his closest advisers, that the initiative had come from the highest level. He added that, given the vast reaches of the Soviet Union, the enormous distances, and the various jurisdictions, it would be a good idea to think about reforming the centralized system. Inosemtsev asked me for my opinion.

Let me point out once again that we had long since gotten into the habit of discussing things frankly, concretely, and honestly. I replied that I could only welcome this new direction. It was hard enough maintaining any overview of West Germany despite its small geographic size and its clearly structured economy. How much more difficult it must be, I said, for the Soviet Union, with its 285 million inhabitants, its huge and diverse industrial areas, its territories under development, and its constantly changing conditions. If these new ideas could be put through, if a less centralized system could delegate authority and decision-making to local people, then the resulting dismantling of the bureaucracy could only lead to a more productive economy.

I added: "In my opinion, however, this is tantamount to placing a mental atomic bomb under the desk."

My interlocutors were dumbstruck. They asked me what I meant, and I explained. If I had learned one thing in all those years, it was this: Centralized planning obligates people to focus rigidly on plans and quotas. Not only is deviation never practiced, but acting on one's own judgment is strictly outlawed. If responsibility is now delegated, however, if decision-making is decentralized, then people will inevitably think for themselves and reach their own critical conclusions. These developments cannot be limited to specific areas and activities. And not only will the functionaries be affected, but so will everyone involved in the overall production process. They will immediately have to share in thinking and decision-making and even to swerve from the given plan in order to increase productivity. This, in turn, would train them to act in a way that, as far as I could tell, the Soviet system has never permitted or regarded as valid. But if these innovations are introduced, they will inevitably alter the Soviet system, and there is no way of forecasting the ultimate consequences of this fundamental revamping even on a social level. "That is why I spoke of a 'mental atomic bomb' under your desk.''* The faces I was gazing at were pensive.

Barely four years after Andropov, Mikhail Gorbachev set into motion the system of thinking for oneself and acting on one's own initiative without waiting to hear from Moscow. On October 1, 1987, in Murmansk, the Soviet premier spoke about this issue to the workers and the leadership elite of the Kola Peninsula. In his speech he exhorted the audience: "Don't wait for orders from Moscow! Moscow is far away! If you can see what's wrong, if you can see the best way of reaching the established goal, then act. Use your own judgment.''

Still and all, in observing the economic apparatus, I have been able to note little if any progress along those lines. The "new thinking" is openly discussed in newspapers and magazines, on radio and TV, however, and I am surprised by the extent of the debates. For years I have known how well informed my Soviet interlocutors are, how curious they are, and anything but bashful in conversations. Yet they candidly admit that they don't have a reliable overview of the changes now taking place in their country. For the foreign observer it is fascinating to watch a rather acquiescent society becoming dynamic and starting to tackle previously alien tasks and structural innovations.

Let me cite an example. In March 1989 the first so-called German-Soviet forum was held in Bonn. (It is slated to meet every two years in order to discuss general problems of cooperation in the most disparate areas, from disarmament to church issues and the treatment of Soviet-Russian citizens of a German background, with the accent on economic and ecological questions.) The meeting was attended by high-ranking experts, mostly scholars, scientists, and members of the Academy of Sciences. Their mission was to come up with scientifically founded concepts and proposals for government action and to establish standards and methods for carrying them out.

* Such a "bomb" was to explode in 1989, although not in the Soviet Union but in China. The leadership there had started a uncontrollable sociopolitical chain reaction because of its one-sided liberalization of its economy.

When we asked where the future Soviet economy and society might conceivably be heading, the answer was: "We want a 'socialist market economy.' By focusing on the market we hope to meet the needs of consumers. We expect to gain experience in competition, performance orientation, innovativeness, a greater individual willingness to assume responsibility, and an increased awareness of quality and expenses." The adjective "socialist" meant, they said, that the humanitarian achievements of the system could not be tossed aside.

In this context I pointed out that such humanitarianism was precisely the goal of a *Sozialmarktwirtschaft*, or "socially responsible market economy," which, I told them, could offer many examples of its ability to work for the good of the citizen, or rather the consumer, and to achieve the humanitarian ends that were expected of a "socialist market economy." Here, admittedly, I came up against a barrier: the Soviet reluctance to acknowledge the benefits of "capitalism" after so many years of excoriating it. Dr. Yuri Andreyev, the intelligent director of the Academy of Sciences, explained to me that the Soviets were now accepting the "market" as a "product of civilization"; however, they are unable or, more precisely, unwilling to see that the "market" is not only the instrument of an efficient economic system but, almost inevitably, *the* form of economic organization taken on by free citizens who are in a position to decide for themselves. Nevertheless, dialectics helps people get over the ideological biases of the past.

Naturally, the bold conceptions of the Soviet speakers, no matter how appealingly presented, revealed inconsistencies that emphasized the internal contradiction. No conclusions were therefore reached concerning the central issue of private property. Still, they conceded that within twenty-five years the system they were striving for would resemble that of Sweden more than West Germany. We were impressed by the earnest and emphatic approach of the open-minded leaders in politics, science, and scholarship. These people wanted to get away from the realm of mere ideas and noncommittal demands; they wanted to translate the "new thinking" into concrete policies and actions.

These efforts are also obvious in the Soviet monetary structure—perhaps the greatest and most difficult challenge facing the reformers. The currency of a nation and the value and importance of its currency in the international financial market play a major role in the self-esteem of that nation and its government. For decades after World War II the U.S. dollar was universally recognized as *the* international standard of value—even by the Soviets, albeit without their enthusiasm or explicit confirmation. Nonetheless, because of the political and military power of the Soviet Union, the area in which a "transferable ruble" was accepted as legal tender reached all the way from Mongolia to Cuba and included the entire realm of a vast region with a total population of 380 million.

It is hard to assess the extent to which the exchange rate between the ruble and each national currency corresponded to their actual values. After all, it was the Soviet government that established the foreign exchange rate of the "transferable ruble," thereby creating an arbitrary exchange ratio for settling accounts between the other COMECON countries and their most important trading partner, the Soviet Union. It takes no great stretch of the imagination to figure out what the Soviet Union did as the leading East European power. Moscow received as high a price as possible for its exports into COMECON countries and as low a price as possible for its imports.

In my talks with Soviet negotiators, something very important soon dawned on me. Whether they worked for a government bank or a government purchasing agency (usually the Foreign Trade Ministry), they were always deeply interested in the latest exchange rate of the dollar and the current price of gold. We shouldn't forget that next to South Africa, the Soviet Union is the world's largest producer and supplier of gold. In this way, through its bank branches in Zurich, London, and Singapore, Moscow influences the fluctuation of gold prices (not without consulting South Africa, no doubt). And it exerts its influence not only by selling gold but also by buying it, in order to prevent any price collapse.

Every time I arrived in Moscow I could promptly witness how much excitement was caused by the price of gold and the exchange rate of the dollar. No sooner were we driving toward the center of town than the members of the welcoming committee bombarded me with questions about the latest developments in those areas.

The early 1970s brought a crucial change in the currency situation and the ruble. Americans were forced to learn that they had weakened the seemingly invulnerable bastion of their currency, mainly through the financial strains of the war in Vietnam. In August 1971, President Nixon abolished the gold standard; the dollar was no longer backed by gold. Next, in December of that same year, the so-called Smithsonian Agreement canceled the rules established back in 1944 by forty-four members of the United Nations who had met in the small town of Bretton Woods, New Hampshire. Henceforth, the exchange rate of the dollar would be left to the free play of market forces. From now on the central banks of the most important Western powers could stick their oars in—that is, interfere. As a result, during 1972–73 the value of the dollar kept dropping on the international market—a development that was enthusiastically hailed by Moscow. Previously the Soviets, even by their own estimate, had unequivocally given the dollar priority over their own currency; but now, by means of a unilateral action, namely an administrative order, they were in a position to fix the price of the ruble higher than the price of the dollar. No one in Moscow was concerned about market influences.

Understandably this development caused palpable satisfaction in Moscow. I was there shortly after the first reevaluation of the ruble. Stepping into a taxi outside the Hotel National, I asked the driver how much the long ride would cost me. He said five rubles or one dollar. The next day I couldn't help mentioning this incident during a meeting at the central bank. It may not have been exactly considerate of me to dampen the joy the Soviets felt about the higher rate of the ruble, but this happened to be the reality. As in other countries, the cabdriver had quoted the actual market value: A ruble was worth twenty cents.

Nor did this ratio shift much during the next few years. For whatever reason, the Soviets had misgivings about the dollar; in their eyes the West German mark had a more promising future. They were simply looking for an alternative currency. Eventually they thought they had found it in the ECU, the European Currency Unit, even though the latter has as yet failed to provide the most important prerequisites for a genuine—that is, independent—market value. The Soviet goal is still the full convertibility of the ruble, which means its full acceptance on international financial markets.

This, too, demonstrates a fundamental rethinking. At one time the Soviets never missed an opportunity to vent their annoyance about the international monetary institutions, such as the International Monetary Fund and the World Bank. They considered them to be solidly in the clutches of the capitalists, especially the Americans, and they suspected that the primary goal of these institutions was to exploit the developing and partly developed nations by making them toe the line and keeping them in bondage to the major Western industrial powers. But in its reorientation, Moscow realized the significance of these coordinating organs within the increasingly more complex financial markets. Indeed, General Secretary Gorbachev made this clear in a symbolic act: In a letter to President Mitterand of France, who hosted the World Economic Summit of July 1989 in Paris, Gorbachev stated that the Soviet Union wished to be an integral part of international economic relations and to be open to comprehensive cooperation, and toward this end it expected help from the developed industrial powers. Ideological qualms had yielded to sober pragmatism.

"If you can't beat 'em, join 'em." This was the thoroughly

Marxist aspect of the new Soviet realism. The other aspect went further: It dawned on the Soviets that economic self-sufficiency cannot prosper in the realm of Communism. The progressive economic intertwining of the nations and the steadily growing interdependence—in short, the globalization of economic (and political) opportunity as well as risk—have brought a new outlook to the Soviet Union. Its trend is now toward rapprochement with the international monetary markets and their institutions. Every day these markets move as much as $300 billion, either as currency, as capital procurement, or as sheer speculation. This tremendous might has not failed to make an impact on the Kremlin's economic thinkers.

In theory, they have long since championed the full convertibility of the ruble as an unconditional prerequisite for Soviet economic progress. I have repeatedly discussed this matter with bankers, planning commission members, and scholars in Moscow. The extent to which Soviet experts were dealing with the issue was obvious years ago during a discussion at the International Economic Institute, which is known in Moscow as the "window to the West." In talking about the general currency situation, I marveled at how well informed the professors and the students were and at the detail of their questions. This is truly an institute for forging cadres of talented and well-educated leaders for the Soviets' international business activities.

The ongoing reform efforts in Moscow produce bold new ideas. There is talk of a "gold ruble": Moscow would make it convertible for special purposes, especially abroad, by backing it with gold and raw materials. This notion is just one of many. The scholars are very impatient, they keep throwing more and more suggestions into the debate. Practitioners are more hard-headed; they know the difficulties involved.

More than ever, Moscow sees price reforms as a vital and crucial condition for economic recovery. Only a free pricing system can guarantee a balance between supply and demand as well as a realistic buying-power parity in trade with market-economy countries. As long as the Soviet administration fixes the price of a small car at ten thousand rubles and a two-pound loaf of bread at ten kopeks, any parity in purchasing power is unthinkable. If such price ratios continue, no free exchange rates can emerge because no one will be interested in the ruble. Hence, no balanced rate can materialize in the free currency market. The ruble will be truly convertible only when the currency parities are adjusted to be as close as possible to the parities in buying power.

What the Soviet Union needs first and foremost is to reform its prices; otherwise, it will never succeed in reforming its economy. This path is not without its pitfalls. Moscow will face a gargantuan challenge in launching even a partially free play of supply and demand in a planned economy that has been centralized and state-controlled for decades. Such a radical change would involve unforeseen dangers. Soviet experts are already picturing the following scenario: Food prices and the general cost of living rise drastically; inflation rears its head; unprofitable businesses are forced to close; many workers lose their jobs and plunge into a chasm without a safety net. The Soviet Union and its ethnic groups have never experienced these problems. Halfhearted reforms have led to such desolate economic conditions that far-reaching and hard-hitting measures are unavoidable if perestroika is to stand any chance of success.

Moscow wants to become a full-fledged member of the world market. For years now the Soviets have tried to calculate the advantages of an international division of labor and its possible usefulness for their country. To this end, Moscow has stopped criticizing institutions such as GATT (the General Agreement on Tariffs and Trade), the World Bank, and the International Monetary Fund. Moscow's short-term objective is membership in these institutions, and its long-term objective is to become a partner nation in the World Economic Summit. In any case my talks since the summer of 1989 have led me to believe that in this area the Soviet Union wants to become known for its good behavior.

In the Soviet Union all reform decisions are made within the economic and financial-political arenas. The next chapter will describe how the Soviets felt about the international financial markets just eight years ago. Back then, "convertible ruble" was not a foreign term in Moscow—it was not a term at all.

4·THE "CREDIT WEAPON" AND ITS CONSEQUENCES

A great deal has been said and written about the Soviet Union's credit rating, so I can easily summarize it.

The Soviets are tough negotiators, but once the talks, which are anything but simple, are completed and the terms and implementation criteria of a contract have been agreed upon, Moscow is a reliable debtor, as experience has taught us. Reliable, from a banker's perspective, means that the borrower takes the loan seriously, repaying both interest and capital. The Soviets are not just serious about a debt, they are downright punctilious—concerned as they are about their political reputation. In terms of its resources and capabilities, the Soviet Union, compared with other debtor nations, remains in a favorable position. This is still true today even though in the fall of 1988, Gorbachev, after wavering for a long time, released amazingly huge amounts of currency credits for imports. But we'll get back to that later.

In 1981 the Soviet Union was taken aback by the news of Poland's debts to the Western world. The Western countries themselves were shocked upon hearing the amount: some $28 billion was owed to banks and other creditors. I tolerated bitter rebukes in Moscow. The Bonn government and the banks, I was told, were allowing Poland to overextend itself, and the Soviets were at a loss to understand such generosity. They were quite familiar with how meticulously the German banks investigated loan applications; they knew how thoroughly they probed into an applicant's solvency. Since the West had to be well aware of Poland's dubious credit standing, there could be only one explanation: The loans had gone through for a different reason. I was asked reproachfully whether West Germany, and indeed the entire Western world, was trying to get the People's Republic of Poland to break with COMECON and the Warsaw Pact.

These charges, which I had to field as a proxy for all creditors, so to speak, left me feeling rather uneasy. I knew for a fact that the West German administration, which was headed by Helmut Schmidt, had urged the West German banks to grant Poland another loan. They had already lent huge sums to Poland during the 1970s, in part because of its copper shipments. Next to coal, copper was its largest export item; in fact, Poland was the sole European source of copper. In 1980 Helmut Schmidt was planning to visit his friend Edward Gierek, secretary general of the Polish Workers' Party. Gierek also had close ties with Schmidt's friend Giscard d'Estaing, who was then president of the French republic. At that time I was chairman of the German Banking Association, and Count Otto Lambsdorff, who was Helmut Schmidt's minister of economy, pressed me to finally put through this additional loan. He said it was in the best interests of both the Federal German government and the Soviet Union. As far as I can recall, this was the only time in my professional life that the West German government ever coaxed a bank to reach such a decision.

These sums were relatively tiny compared with Poland's overall indebtedness, which had already reached gigantic proportions. And naturally the motive for okaying these new loans was not what the Soviets later inferred. I kept reassuring them during our talks in Moscow when I countered their bitter accusations. The idea that anyone wanted to drive a wedge between Poland and the other Soviet allies was pure fabrication. Rather, as I explained in Moscow, both West Germany and the Soviet Union would benefit from restoring Poland's solvency by helping out its export industry. Poland, I said, was an important trading partner for West Germany.

Finally, after hours of intense debate, the Soviets and I agreed that both sides should abstain from any further rebukes and we should do our best to work toward a constructive approach to Poland's debt situation. But a vestige of distrust remained, a distrust that is directly linked to the Soviet sense of being in danger. This paranoia cannot be explained rationally. For the Soviet Union, Poland is an important buffer zone between it and the West.

Now the Soviets tossed a different argument into the ring: "If we cannot reproach West Germany and the lender banks, we must nevertheless criticize the Americans." Back then, in 1981, Moscow's nervousness was quite tangible. The Soviets were agitated and insecure. They asked me how I viewed the matter and what advice I could offer them.

I recommended that the People's Republic of Poland be allowed to rejoin the International Monetary Fund,* of which, after all, Poland had been a co-founder. As a full member Poland would once again be helped in both word and deed, and if certain stipulations were fulfilled, with credit as well. The Soviet leadership might be displeased by the fact that Poland would have to agree to certain conditions, because the International Monetary Fund, observing neutrality and enjoying an international reputation, would impress the Warsaw government to the detriment of Marxist ideology.

---

* The International Monetary Fund (IMF) is composed of 151 member nations. In the IMF, unlike the UN, the major Western industrial nations have the majority vote. The IMF is led by a governing board and an executive directorate. It makes sure that fair exchange rates are maintained, insures sufficient liquidity of the world's money supply, and works toward avoiding currency restrictions that hamper world trade. In addition, it has an emergency fund to aid nations in balance-of-payment difficulty and keeps watch that nations requesting such help take necessary and agreed-upon measures designed to overcome their payment difficulties.

This idea give my interlocutors food for thought. I noticed how hard they were struggling; they were trying to figure out whether such a recommendation was feasible. The next day I was told the idea was not possible. The Soviets believed that the International Monetary Fund was clearly dominated by the United States; consequently, Poland could not be allowed to rejoin as a full member.

For me this was yet another example of the Soviets' latent distrust of the West. Their anxieties could be felt whenever Western behavior seemed to provide a rationale—on the basis of stereotypical prejudices about the Soviet Union. In the course of my work I repeatedly observed this troublesome give-and-take. Throughout years of mutual experiences in negotiating and settling major projects, it was difficult to get the ear of the other side, to listen to one another, and finally to dismantle suspicions and misinterpretations piece by piece.

At around the same time I was also having detailed talks about the Polish situation with Vladimir Alkhimov, the head of Gosbank. We had negotiated various projects for ten long years, and I had a very high regard for him. He was extremely intelligent and sensitive, and I was impressed time and again by his refined attitude. It was only later that I found out that Alkhimov had been decorated as a Hero of the Soviet Union for his wartime courage at the siege of Leningrad. One evening he invited me to the Bolshoi Theater, and after the performance we talked on a very personal level, expressing our concern about the developments in Poland.

The circle of high-ranking functionaries that we felt could speak competently and responsibly about Poland's credit dilemma was extremely small. There were few Soviets experienced enough to work toward solving such a problem within an international framework.

Mr. Alkhimov described how upset and critical even ordinary Soviet people were about Poland's behavior. "Our citizens, who work hard day after day, do not understand why there are so many demonstrations in Poland—and not only on weekends, as in West Germany, but on workdays as well. Our people simply do not sympathize."

I ought to mention that Moscow's anxiety about the buffer zone was so profound that it made Poland an outright nonrepayable gift of billions of dollars to stimulate its economy. But the Polish quandary also caused agitation and nervousness among the banks and the governments of the Western lender nations. Ultimately, in 1981, the international debt crisis originated in Poland, spiraling to astronomical proportions, far beyond the original estimates.

In the spring of 1982, Caspar Weinberger, the newly appointed American secretary of defense, visited West Germany. He declared that we now had an extremely favorable advantage in regard to the Eastern Bloc and Moscow. Since Poland was part of the Eastern Bloc, the creditors should now demand full repayment of all loans by an analogous application of the so-called cross-default clause. This clause stipulates that an (international) corporation is to be treated as a single debtor. In other words: The corporation is obligated to maintain the solvency of every last component of its entire structure. It therefore has to pay back, in their entirety, any and all sums lent to the corporation and/or any of its entities if even just one entity, no matter how insignificant, falls behind in its payment schedule.

The Americans were unmistakably thinking along those very lines. Weinberger concluded that the West now had a new weapon to deploy against the Soviet Union. "We can't get at them by military means and perhaps not by political means, but now we have the credit weapon and we ought to use it."

At times, West Germany, including the Berlin-based Federal Supervisory Office for Credit Activities, did in fact view COMECON's overall debt situation as a corporate indebtedness. Had the cross-default clause been invoked, a default by any one Eastern Bloc country would have meant that automatically all the international debts of the entire Eastern Bloc could have been called. In all likelihood this would have made the entire COMECON

area insolvent. The clause was not invoked, but the episode
shows how tense and hostile the climate was between the superpowers and between the West and the East in general. I experienced these tensions personally for many long years.

Ronald Reagan was elected president of the United States. As
usual when a new administration comes to power in a Western
country, Moscow proceeded to do thorough research. The Soviets
wanted to assess the new American administration correctly and
then issue appropriate phraseology to its millions of functionaries
throughout the vast Soviet domain. This was always done for
every new West German chancellor and certainly for new presidents of the United States of America, the most important country outside the Socialist world. The jargon describing Ronald
Reagan went as follows: a war-mongering, saber-rattling president
who would arm the West in order to intimidate the peace-loving
Soviet Union.

During the period of our difficult Yamal pipeline negotiations,
which were criticized by the United States, I was inspecting a
compressor plant in Leningrad. Suddenly I spotted a huge poster
with the caption: OUR ANSWER IS OUR WORK, MR. PRESIDENT! Washington had prohibited major American shipments of items crucial
to the manufacture of highly effective compressors for the pipeline. Frustrated and angry, the Soviets told me: "We were looking
forward to a sensible international division of labor, but that has
been denied us, so we'll just make our own compressors." Which
they did, although the Soviet version performed less effectively.

Thus, the Polish situation, with the conclusions drawn in the
West, created a Soviet hypersensitivity that could be felt for
years, and perhaps is still being felt today. Once again I was shown
how greatly the Soviet paranoia is nourished not only by historical traumas but also by concrete events.

Moscow's hypersensitivity toward the West could also be observed in another area: the Soviet reputation in the capitalist

world. Let me recall an incident that strikes me as characteristic. In 1975 the international financial and capital markets were clearly growing more and more interested in the solvency criteria of the debtor nations. While the Western governments openly revealed their crucial economic statistics as they had in the past, the Soviet Union refused to publish its basic figures. Either it distrusted and disapproved of these markets, or else it was flaunting superpower arrogance. Needless to say, the international press began to wonder how credit-worthy the Soviet Union really was; anyone who conceals something has something to hide. These conjectures were voiced in serious international newspapers, which ran headlines attacking the solvency of the Soviet Union.

At that time, Deputy Premier Nikolai Tikhonov, who eventually became head of state, was in charge of creating the new Five-Year Plan. He asked to see me at the Kremlin, and here he declared that these false and damaging opinions about the Soviet Union were due to our behavior—meaning West Germany and Deutsche Bank—and he even blamed me personally.

I ought to pause and tell the reader about Mr. Tikhonov. This confidant of Leonid Brezhnev came from the Ukraine. A very stern man with a gaunt, almost ascetic appearance, he was always extremely surly. He acted like the austere prior of a monastery who vigilantly punishes the least peccadillo within his jurisdiction.

During our meeting I made every effort to rebuff his accusations. When he asked me directly about the Soviet Union's credit standing on an international level, I replied that admittedly it was "undervalued" in the West. But this was only because the Soviet Union did not behave like a normal debtor involved in the international credit market. Ultimately this market, on which West Germany had no influence, followed its own rules, applying comparable criteria to any credit rating, which meant that a country's total credit picture had to be taken into consideration. This included basic economic data such as the movement of capital, the conduct of the central bank, and especially the currency reserves in connection with the balance of payment and the trade balance. Yet the Soviet Union refused to supply such information. It was my personal opinion, I told him, that the Soviets were to be judged positively on the basis of those credit criteria, but since Moscow refused to make the required data available, it was not surprising that the international market was dominated by voices critical of the Soviet Union. I then pointed out that the Soviet Union was the world's greatest gold producer next to South Africa. This was a special factor in the Soviet credit picture. Not only did the Soviet Union possess vast and accessible gold reserves, but experts had located gold deposits that could be mined in the foreseeable future.

Mr. Tikhonov listened to me very attentively, but his face did not grow any milder. To alleviate the oppressive grimness of the conversation, I switched to the offensive and said with a friendly expression: "Since Soviet data is lacking, Mr. Premier, the West can only guess at the size of the Soviet gold reserves." I gave him a figure, adding that roughly the same amount had been computed by the CIA and by other Western countries. "Now if I take this amount of available gold and deduct the sum that the Soviet Union owes to the United States for grain shipments, then the balance no doubt could easily cover your country's outstanding currency debts."

Tikhonov's eyes bored into me with a touch of surprise. I felt like a schoolboy who has been caught making an error in arithmetic. But to my amazement, he said abruptly: "Herr Christians, this is extremely interesting. Please continue to keep me informed."

It was my turn to be surprised. I would never have dreamed that this important politician, the man in charge of the Five-Year Plan, could be in the dark about the size of his country's gold reserves. A short time later I related this incident to Dr. Otmar Emminger, vice president of the German Federal Reserve Bank (Bundesbank) and an internationally recognized expert on gold and currency matters. He replied that he had discussed this very same issue with the Soviets, including Mr. Tikhonov, and he had also had the impression that Mr. Tikhonov was truly in the dark. Even today I cannot imagine that he was uninformed; he may simply have been trying to put one over on me.

Throughout our many encounters I saw stern Mr. Tikhonov smile only once, and that was at the celebration of his seventy-fifth birthday when he happened to be in West Germany. A small group of us had gathered at the residence of the Soviet ambassador Vladimir S. Semyonov. It was 1981, and we were already negotiating the huge Yamal pipeline loan. When I wished Mr. Tikhonov many happy returns, a smile flitted across his face, which then quickly froze up again. Next, Tikhonov made it absolutely clear to me that the interest rates I was asking were completely unacceptable. He called it capitalist profiteering and said he felt compelled to admonish me to control myself. Since this was not the place to delve any deeper into the topic, I put on a poker face. Once again, I had learned a thing or two from negotiating with the Soviets.

5 · PROBLEMS FOR THE YAMAL PIPELINE

Later on, the Soviets praised the Yamal pipeline as the accomplishment of the century. Its size is indeed enormous, and huge sums of money were required to build it. Not surprisingly, credit of this magnitude had to be weighed carefully and required some hard negotiating. It took us nearly three years to work out an agreement with the Soviets, and three of those years were also under the shadow of politics.

How did this project of the century come about? In December 1979, ten years after my first trip to Moscow and twelve days before Soviet troops marched into Afghanistan, I was asked by Moscow to come to the Soviet capital without delay. They said the matter was urgent.

On December 11, 1979, Vladimir S. Semyonov, the Soviet ambassador to Bonn, asked me whether I could go to Moscow. I replied that my schedule was so tight during the next few days I was unable to leave, if only because of the difficult airline connections. I would have to charter a plane, fly the shortest route possible to Moscow, and return the same way, but that would require special clearance, which in those days was a very tedious process. Mr. Semyonov promised to get me the clearance.

I was given a private jet. Flying it to Moscow was also very tedious, unlike today. A Soviet navigator had to fly from Moscow to Düsseldorf, board the private jet with us, and then return with us to Düsseldorf. After plowing through all kinds of red tape, they finally spirited me to Moscow on December 13.

There I was welcomed by N. K. Baibakov, the head of Gosplan. His spacious office was very impressive, with the high walls all around his desk covered by gigantic charts depicting the Soviet Union's natural resources. Mr. Baibakov did not fail to emphasize that these were "classified documents of the Red Army." They showed the existing deposit sites of the raw materials—oil and gas—as well as the existing pipelines. I realized that the Soviet Union already had the world's largest pipeline network for oil and gas. Then, pointing to the gas fields near the Arctic Circle, Mr. Baibakov said that the Soviet Union wanted to build its first pipeline to Western Europe in order to provide urgently needed natural gas, especially to West Germany but also to several other Western European countries. He went through a series of arguments, politely elucidating each one in great detail. He soon made it clear, however, that the Soviets felt they were in a favorable starting position. Since they regarded our primary energy needs as very pressing, they were going to be quite demanding about the basic terms.

As we began the first round of negotiations, I knew that their resources were considerable indeed. The Soviets had a wealth of raw materials and an enormous potential, which nature had provided gratis, so to speak. And I managed to convince myself of their riches not only by viewing those graphic charts in Mr. Baibakov's office on that December day in 1979 but because I had already traveled through many areas of the Soviet Union, partly in order to study their natural resources *in situ.* What impressed me most of all in that vast domain were the gigantic deposits of primary energy—gas, petroleum, brown coal, and hard coal, as well as water power, especially in Siberia. Today, West Germany is the biggest Western customer for Soviet gas, so it was natural for me to take a closer look at the area of production from which my country would be the first to benefit.

I had been offered a charter flight to Novi Urengoi, the gas metropolis of the world. We flew via Tiumen, the major Western Siberian crossroads for oil shipments. In 1800 when the German writer August von Kotzebue was banished to Siberia, he wrote about Tiumen after passing through. And in 1829, when Alexander von Humboldt explored the eastern parts of the Russian empire at the request of Czar Nicholas I, he also visited Tiumen.

In the early 1980s, Novi Urengoi had some thirty thousand inhabitants. With its one tarred road, it resembled a gold rush town in the American West—though with a less hospitable climate. The average age of the population, which was expected to triple by the end of the century, was just under thirty, with a distinct surplus of men. Lured by relatively high salaries and special vacations, the young people sign up for the not-exactly-pleasant jobs in the gas fields. Many of the recruits are students who hope that this sacrifice will get them into Moscow's institutes of higher education.

Despite tough conditions and a modest, if not bleak way of life, the morale, I was glad to note, was high. The leaders—engineers and factory directors—were proud and self-confident because of the importance of their work. Their attitude was understandable. By then they were already producing 650 billion cubic yards of gas annually, and the quota was to rise to 1.1 trillion by 1990. The people extract the gas from the barren soil of the tundra, which is solid only in winter, and they sell it for valuable Western currency. I was impressed not only by their devotion and their sharp judgment but also by their self-assurance when dealing with the swollen bureaucracy in Moscow—and that was years before Gorbachev.

I found the same situation throughout my Soviet travels. The behavior of the people and also the functionaries changed noticeably the farther they were from Moscow. They weren't insubordinate by any means, but their conduct was less uniform, and they didn't prattle rhetoric. I especially liked the Siberians for their directness and their robust vitality. The vodka, which is somewhat stronger in Siberia, did its part in fueling our exchange of opinions. Nowhere did I see such richly laden tables as in these barren surroundings—which showed how well the supply lines functioned.

When I think back on twenty years of negotiations and conversations throughout the Soviet Union, vodka has an outstanding place in my memories. During the war when German soldiers were in Russia, the "noble water"—potato alcohol filtered twice through charcoal—had proved to be a great pick-me-up. Subsequently, the Soviet curtailment of vodka was a decisive break with tradition. Depriving the Russians of vodka is tantamount to denaturing their minds.

Granted, there had always been occasions for indulging lavishly in alcohol even at lunch. At such times escape was out of the question. Since I was under constant observation, I couldn't just pour the vodka into a vase or under the table. And afterward I usually felt sick or at least uncertain whether I was up to negotiating anymore that day. But despite all those tribulations, I have come to the sobering conclusion that our recent, vodkaless get-togethers with the Russians are friendlier on an official level but poorer in substance—and this applies to both sides.

In the Soviet Union one seldom has the impression that the vodka curtailment has had any permanent success. At first it was mainly the wives who hailed the restriction, but private stills have now skyrocketed into a bootleg industry to the tune of millions. So once again vodka is enthusiastically imbibed; productivity is as low as ever, sugar has to be rationed, and the government is losing out on a large amount of tax revenues.

Seated in spacious, comfortably appointed helicopters, I flew across the endless tundra fields near Novi Urengoi and all the way to the Arctic Circle. By doing this I managed to form an image of the development and transportation methods. We landed at interesting points of the gigantic network where we were given precise briefings. I was able to convince myself of how swiftly the pipeline was advancing as one huge Mannesmann section was welded to the next.

The Soviets were proud that they had outdone the Americans in welding technology. In fact, they told us that their American competitors were trying to obtain a license for the Soviet process. What distinguishes the Soviet fusion method is that it dispenses with the time-consuming tightening of the welding seam, making the operation speedier. The entire mobile workshop was limited to an enormous Japanese pipe-hoisting jack and a portable generator. The pipeline, flexible but with solid seams, wound its way across the treeless tundra like a giant dragon.

What makes Novi Urengoi so fascinating is that its gas deposit is not only one of the largest in the world but also one of the richest in quality. At present it still covers primarily the Soviets' own growing demands, but in the coming decades gas will also be sent to Western Europe through a jumbo network of thousands of miles of pipelines.

Siberia is known as Russia's treasure house, especially in regard to primary energy. The lignite deposits in central and southern Siberia—for instance, all around Kansk and Achinsk—run through a territory of 27,250 square miles, twice the size of Switzerland. I visited this coal-mining area as well. Because of its enormous size they first had me view it from the air.

The airplane was a small three-engine Yak jet that could hold fewer than twenty passengers. In the 1960s the Yak was expected to become a hot export item, but it proved far too expensive to make and to operate, far too noisy, and ecologically unsound. The Yak sufficed for our purposes, however; it was comfortable and also maneuverable enough to provide an aerial overview of the tremendous coal basin and the strip mines.

I was already acquainted with the lignite mining area west of the Rhine, between Cologne and Aachen. There, the biggest dredging shovels in the world clear the overlay shelf to a depth of a thousand or thirteen hundred feet in order to get at the coal.

Here, in Kansk and Achinsk, the shelf was only about fifty feet thick. If you descend into the open pit, the shelf looks like a gigantic chocolate cake topped with vanilla cream. The lower edge of the yellowish overburden lies clean—as if sliced by a kitchen knife—on the dark chocolate of the coal seam. The dredger, which is the size of a building, resembles a dinosaur. Its unbelievable shovel, able to hold up to a hundred tons, tips its load into gondola cars.

The future plan is to mix the brown coal with methanol and sluice it through the pipeline directly to the consumer. But here we come up against one of the biggest structural problems in the Soviet Union: the weakness of the transportation system. Given the vast distances, which far exceed those in the United States, the Soviets keep wondering: Do we bring the raw materials to the people and their processing capacities—that is, to areas with fully developed infrastructures—or do we bring the people to the mining areas and build production facilities there? So far the Soviets have followed both routes but with a slight emphasis on the former.

This is also true in regard to the cheap electricity produced in Siberia. As an example, the Yenisey River is one of the biggest in Siberia. It feeds two hydroelectric plants that are relatively close together. I visited the newer and larger one, with its 6,300 megawatt capacity. European power plants pale in comparison, as do Aswan in Egypt and storage lakes in Argentina and Paraguay. (Itaipu in Brazil, with its 12,300 megawatts, and the Grand Coulee in the U.S. with 12,000 megawatts, are exceptions.) Only a tiny percentage of the electricity produced in central Siberia can be used locally. Not too far from the power plant is Krasnoyarsk, a modern industrial city with over a million inhabitants. It keeps growing and growing, while expanding its industrial capacity. Its climate is a lot more pleasant than that of, say, Novi Urengoi, and cheap power makes for a comparatively high standard of living. The city offers a certain degree of modern comfort as well as sports and culture. I was also shown a special kind of wheat that thrives in the brief summer season.

The Soviets are persistent in their efforts to conquer Siberia, their treasure house, and to populate it on a modern level. They are aided by the Amur-Baikal-Magistrale railroad line (now eighteen hundred miles long) that runs parallel to the old Trans-Siberian Railroad of the czars. In the 1970s, when construction began on the railroad, the official propaganda hailed it as a great pioneering feat. On trips to the Far East that had taken days, several hundred miles were eliminated, shortening the trip by several hours. New sources of raw materials, including Siberia's gigantic lumber reserves, would be tapped and linked to the transportation network. However, the populace was not told that the new railroad line also had a strategic importance. In the sixties the Soviets were already experiencing tensions with their Chinese neighbors; there were even some skirmishes on the Ussuri River—which meant that Moscow had to provide a more secure supply route for its troops on the Soviet-Chinese border.

I've gotten a bit off the track, however. Let's leave a remote Siberia and return to a noisy Moscow—to the office of Mr. Baibakov, the head of Gosplan. We discussed the Soviet raw material reserves and the possibility of delivering primary energy to the West, including West Germany. Our meeting was extremely informative, and it ended on a very personal note. Mr. Baibakov was getting on in years, and I asked him how he managed to keep so fit despite his enormous work load. He told me it was due to his consumption of home-grown chicory. Going over to a cabinet, he handed me a large tube of what he called Baibakov-made chicory. He predicted that if I consumed it regularly, I would live a long, healthy life.

A short time later I was reminded of our meeting but for different, less humane reasons. The Soviet invasion of Afghanistan had changed the international situation in one swoop. Not only the Western democracies but also the Third World nations were outraged and angry at this unexpected aggression. Relations with the Soviet Union had taken a new turn. Plainly, the Soviet government had not expected this negative worldwide reaction. At first the Soviets offered no plausible excuse for the invasion, but eventually they decided on "friendly help in response to urgent pleas from Afghanistan" in order to "forestall a military action by the United States."

During my visit to Moscow several days before the invasion, I agreed to continue negotiations in January 1980. Their resumption was to be observed, along with a change of management at our Moscow office, at a reception, which the Soviets loved. On special occasions we would invite all the functionaries we dealt with at ministries and other agencies and regale them with a buffet flown in by Lufthansa. All sorts of goodies were served: German draft beer in stone crocks, Bavarian white sausages, pretzels, and whatever else southern Germany had to offer. From earlier parties we knew how greatly our Soviet guests enjoyed these treats.

Now we wondered if we should honor the invitation we had extended prior to the invasion of Afghanistan. Various international meetings were canceled in January 1980. Jacques Chaban-Delmas, president of the French assembly, who happened to be in Moscow, left the capital in protest. West German Chancellor Helmut Schmidt met with French President Valéry Giscard d'Estaing in Paris to discuss what steps should be taken against the Soviet Union. They resolved to leave it at a "final" warning.

At Deutsche Bank we decided that I would fly to Moscow for the planned negotiations but reduce the four- or five-day visit to an absolute minimum—about a day and a half. We conspicuously canceled our reception for the new management even though over eight hundred people had been invited. This caused a big commotion in Moscow. Furthermore, I asked Ambassador Semyonov to make sure that during my stay in Moscow I would not be quoted by the press or interviewed on television without my permission. Television was especially important because the Soviets were understandably intent on mellowing the tremendously negative impact that their invasion had made on the world and also on their own population. Moscow had to make a point of presenting Western politicians and businessmen to the tele-viewing public in order to counteract the impression that foreign countries were boycotting the Soviet Union. I was told that some West German businessmen had gone along with the Soviet plan and had given interviews on TV, but I flatly refused to let myself be exploited as a convenient witness for the "harmlessness" of the Afghanistan adventure.

I had always been able to speak very openly and constructively with Mr. Semyonov, the Soviet ambassador to Bonn, and he instantly agreed to my request. He was puzzled, however, when I called him back two days later to inquire whether he had trans-mitted my wish to the protocol officers in Moscow. After confirming that he had done so, he asked me why I was so distrustful.

When I arrived in Moscow as scheduled, I was met by an acquaintance, a senior official at the central bank. I asked him to confirm my urgent request and the agreement I had made with Mr. Semyonov. A bit later I was asked whether I would be willing to meet with Premier Tikhonov the next morning. I replied: "If that is what Mr. Tikhonov wishes, I will be available, but I repeat that this is at his request and that no information about this meeting is to be made public without my permission." I was assured that my request would be granted.

The next morning I was standing in front of Mr. Tikhonov, who looked as grim as ever. After greeting me in an aggressive tone, he asked me how reliable the West Germans were in observing contracts. I was taken aback by his question. He thereupon declared: "I am forced to ask you this question because we were notified yesterday that the West German chancellor and the British prime minister have managed to stop the delivery of Common Market butter to us despite an agreement between the Soviet

Union and the administration of the European Community." I had to admit that I was surprised by the news; I had heard nothing about it.

We had other and more important problems, however: We were supposed to negotiate the exchange of huge deliveries of Soviet gas for an enormous loan. The premier's opening attack was not exactly conducive to a good negotiating climate, so I tried to parry it by joking that I had not come to Moscow to wage a butter war. We should really focus on the important issues. It was left at that, and we then continued talking without letting emotions get in the way.

That evening, as was often the case, I went to the large Kremlin Theater with my counterparts from the central bank. (The telecast sessions of the Supreme Soviet are held in that tremendous auditorium.) They were staging a Prokofiev opera with which I was unfamiliar. The subject was Napoleon's dramatic attack on Moscow, and the performance involved an exorbitant deployment of supernumeraries and scenery. Napoleon rode about on a white horse, issuing orders to his generals amid the spectacular burning of Moscow. I was told that this opera was shown only in the Soviet Union and that the population was still deeply moved by this historic event of 1812.

The retreat of the French was not yet in sight when I was suddenly called from my box and confronted by our Moscow representative, who informed me that my visit with Premier Tikhonov had been meticulously described on the main evening news program telecast at 9:00 P.M. The Soviets had done the very thing that I wanted to avoid. When I returned to my seat, my companion from the central bank noticed how agitated I was. Upon leaving the theater a short time later, I fully expressed my feelings. I said I simply did not understand how the Soviets could have done such a thing after their previous assurances. I told him that I would insist on some form of correction as far as it was possible.

The next morning *Izvestia* ran a story about my visit with Mr.

Tikhonov (among the news from high places, so to speak). The article added that our meeting had taken place at my request—the very wording I had wanted to avoid since my visit had been in response to Mr. Tikhonov's urgent plea. I lodged a second complaint, declaring that these statements violated the agreement we had made with the Soviet ambassador to West Germany, which had been confirmed on my arrival in Moscow; I therefore expected, I said, a correction of that wording.

Greatly annoyed, I left for the airport in order to catch my scheduled flight home. During the drive I managed to buy the latest *Izvestia* (three editions were published every morning). Lo and behold, it said that I had indeed paid a visit to Mr. Tikhonov but it corrected the impression made by the first article that the meeting had been at my request. I was told that no one else had ever obtained such a correction of a Kremlin bulletin.

Nevertheless, I was in for a few more surprises. At Frankfurt Airport a Reuters correspondent was waiting for me. According to him, the news from Moscow was that I had left the city to protest the invasion of Afghanistan. I had to clarify several points: To express our protest we had reduced the length of my stay to a minimum and completely canceled the big reception; I had lodged formal protests against the way my visit had been handled by the Soviet press and television.

I was put on the spot one more time by the Soviet violations of our agreement. Upon my arrival in Moscow, the German television and press people there had told me that because of the tense situation caused by the Afghanistan invasion and the uncertainty about Western reactions, they were very interested in hearing my opinion by the end of my visit. They pointed out that on earlier occasions they had been informed first through Soviet media. That was why they pleaded with me to supply them with firsthand information. Their request was quite reasonable, especially because cooperation between the Soviet and German media left a great deal to be desired. But even though I explicitly promised to keep the German correspondents posted, they again obtained details from Soviet sources. This was really unpleasant for me and created additional annoyance and frustration.

Immediately upon returning to my Düsseldorf office I received a phone call from Vladimir Alkhimov, president of Gosbank and a Soviet cabinet member. He explained that my actions in Moscow had touched off a storm. Now that the matter had been reported on Western radio programs and in newspaper headlines, he was worried that it might jeopardize our years of successful efforts to achieve fruitful cooperation. I replied that I would not let the situation interfere with our talks and that I was prepared to continue negotiating on a sober and professional basis—but only after a recess. The excitement would have time to die down, and we could use the hiatus to figure out how to avoid such irritations in the future.

I knew that Alkhimov always wanted to moderate constructively whenever any difficulties arose. One could rely on him and his negotiating skill. I must emphasize something that I felt very strongly in my talks with Mr. Baibakov: When the tangle of ideological conflicts looks hopeless, personal rapport, individual credibility, and a receptiveness to mutual trust forms a basis for closing a deal involving billions—against all adversity.

Mr. Alkhimov and I refused to be discouraged by what had happened during my Moscow visit in January 1980. Together we achieved our goal.* We had no language problems. Once, when he and Ambassador Semyonov visited me at my home after some critical negotiations, I was deeply impressed by Semyonov's thorough background in German culture and in history.

In those days such personal get-togethers, in which official politics was left outside, were rare. For brief moments we were able to forget that both camps were virtually duty-bound to practice confrontation as a matter of course. I realized how intrinsic this was to official policies when Leonid Brezhnev visited West

* Originally the negotiations began with the Soviets seeking credit of ten billion German marks. Japanese banks offered better conditions and we wound up with three billion marks' worth of business.

Germany in November 1981. During a gala dinner, our chancellor, Helmut Schmidt, gave an extremely impressive speech outlining Bonn's policies on the growing threat of Soviet SS-20 missiles. Brezhnev, on the other hand, was content with spouting the usual dated rhetoric, which sounded more like excuses and involved no constructive ideas. Anyone who had a chance to watch Brezhnev's and Gromyko's stern and rigid faces could not feel exactly hopeful that a policy of détente, which was so often expressed, could ever become a reality.

6·ART AS AN ESCAPE

Ambassador Vladimir S. Semyonov also spoke German well. He was my constant official interlocutor, and we met frequently during his long tenure as Soviet ambassador to Bonn. When he first arrived in Bonn in 1978, I paid him a courtesy call and got to meet not only him but also his wife and youngest daughter. During this visit Semyonov told me that this mission would probably be his last professional assignment. He had long felt close to West Germany—indeed the whole of Germany—and he was planning to devote his activity in Bonn to promoting greater understanding and better relations between our two countries.

Mr. Semyonov had indeed enjoyed a long career in Soviet diplomacy, rising to the position of deputy foreign minister. In 1939 he had been a secretary at Berlin's Soviet embassy when Molotov and Ribbentrop had met on August 23—just a few days before the outbreak of war—to sign the Soviet-German Nonaggression Pact. Mr. Semyonov had also headed the Soviet negotiating team at the SALT I talks in Geneva.* He was the one who negotiated and signed this major treaty with the United States. During a dinner at my home, Mr. Semyonov was asked about

* The SALT I talks, in which the United States and the Soviet Union negotiated on controlling certain nuclear weapons, began in 1969 and concluded with the first Strategic Arms Limitation Treaty in 1972.

SALT I by various industrialists who were very interested in trade with the Soviet Union. Taking a menu, the ambassador quickly outlined the major points of this treaty. His striking way of illustrating the twists and turns of the negotiations and their results was quite impressive.

Something amusing happened at that same meal. One of my guests was Heinz Nixdorf, the West German computer king. In his frank, blunt style he told Mr. Semyonov that he studied to prepare himself for this evening and for the conversation. He had been especially interested in the background of the new Soviet ambassador. In a memo his office had mentioned that Mr. Semyonov "had been among the left-wingers" in Berlin in 1939. Nixdorf's young assistants had obviously confused "Unter den Linden" (a boulevard in Berlin) with "unter den Linken" (among the left-wingers). Mr. Semyonov was thoroughly delighted.

But at times, as I observed, this experienced diplomat could get embarrassed. I called on him several times in early January 1980, which was after the Soviets invaded Afghanistan on December 27, 1979, to have him explain this shocking Soviet aggression against a defenseless country. I wanted to know how he felt about our reaction. Mr. Semyonov offered me some excuses that left me unconvinced, and I said so.

He told me a number of contradictory things several days in a row—slice by slice, as it were. By the time Moscow committed itself to an official statement, the worldwide annoyance had made a lot of headway.

The invasion once again confirmed something that I have often observed. In regard to surprising events that had an impact abroad, the rigidly centralized Soviet Union had a hard time coming up with official rationales that would sound cogent not only to foreigners but also and primarily to its domestic population. There was no free press in the Soviet Union. All it had was the central steering of opinions, formed officially and valid from Brest-Litovsk to Vladivostok. The opinion-makers were unable to change gears quickly, and swift press reaction was not available—

at least in those days. Once an official statement was drafted and approved for nationwide release, it had a very long life. If anything happened that made it necessary to correct or tone down the statement, it was extraordinarily difficult to reformulate it and then have it accepted as the new line throughout the vast Soviet Union. As a result, for people in the farthest regions of the country, it was almost impossible to obtain a competent, up-to-date opinion as long as the official opinion formulated at the distant center remained unavailable.

Conversely, word-of-mouth interpretations of a specific event left their impact on the opinion of the entire country. One example was the episode of the Korean passenger plane that was shot down near Sakhalin in early September 1983. The entire world was justifiably alarmed, but Moscow labeled the flight an obvious case of serious military espionage.

Very soon, however, it was rumored that General Secretary Yuri Andropov had disagreed with the military's overreaction and had censured it accordingly. Since he had resolved long ago to cautiously implement a large-scale détente plan, the incident had supposedly caused him a lot of trouble, with the result that his illness, which was already advanced, became more critical. Supposedly it was because of this that the government did not take more rigorous action. It was said that Andropov's depression about the terrible state of affairs within the government and throughout the country finally contributed to his early death.

At the time of the Sakhalin drama I was in Australia. I had agreed to talk about East-West relations to a large audience in Melbourne. The ensuing discussion quickly focused on that incident, which had upset a lot of people throughout the Pacific. They viewed the downing of the Korean jet as a hostile Soviet act that threatened to entangle this part of the world in the Cold War scenario even though the various populations here had generally considered themselves relatively safe. It was difficult to keep the angry audience calm. My arguments went as follows: "The Soviet Union is obsessed with security. Despite the vastness of their territory, the Soviets are deeply upset by any border violation, whether in their European or in their Asian part, and they instantly retaliate. In my opinion this was a case of aggressive defense, and the worldwide indignation will probably very soon compel the Soviet leaders to view their response as an overreaction. I cannot perceive their act as the start of a hostile threat to your region.''

Eventually, as it turned out, the Soviet leaders acted precisely on the basis of the motives that I had described.

But to get back to Ambassador Semyonov: He had a very likable side, which often helped us to deal with serious conflicts. In those days our conversation would frequently reach an impasse, and whenever that happened we would switch to a discussion about art. He knew that I had been collecting prerevolutionary Russian art for a long time, and he, too, was an avid collector. When he and Vladimir Alkhimov of Gosbank visited my home in Meerbusch, we had an opportunity to discuss the Russian avant-garde collection that I was in the process of putting together. About ten years earlier, when I was entertaining some Soviet bankers, they were at a loss to understand why I was concentrating on Russian paintings from the period before and right after the revolution. One of my guests even told a member of my staff (he clearly wanted to spare his host's feelings) that I certainly could afford something better.

I will come back to the long and arduous road to new recognition that these artists had to travel after 1924 when they were banned by Stalin. For now, let me simply mention that for a Soviet functionary, Mr. Semyonov had an unusually rich and varied private art collection. He showed it publicly with his fine catalogue. When asked about his collection, he never failed to point out that this was only a fraction of what he owned and that he had many more paintings in Moscow. Extravagant behavior was and still is possible within the Marxist-Bolshevik system, but here it was expressed freely, with both charm and expertise.

On the other hand, whenever our discussions became too

heated and we wanted to avoid an all-out argument, Semyonov would take me by the arm and lead me through the spacious rooms of his residence. He usually managed to show me a new painting and explain it to me. Our tensions were eased so thoroughly that I was able to leave on friendly terms.

That was what happened in 1983 when American Pershing II missiles were being considered for West Germany. Mr. Semyonov had told me repeatedly that if the Bonn government stuck to its decision, it would have serious consequences for our economic relations, which I, too, had been resolutely promoting. Shortly before the crucial parliamentary debate over the missiles, Mr. Semyonov came to my office in Düsseldorf. We had agreed to discuss ways of "expanding cultural relations between our two countries." Our immediate goal was an exchange of art exhibits, but the topic was put on the back burner. Mr. Semyonov was obviously a lot more concerned about the Pershings. When I refused to go along with his arguments, he blurted out in almost comical despair: "Now really, Herr Christians, do you honestly believe that the Soviet Union wants to destroy Düsseldorf with its SS-20 missiles?" In my opinion that was not the point, I replied. General Secretary Brezhnev had told Chancellor Helmut Schmidt that no further missiles would be set up in the Soviet Union; but despite all his assurances, a new and ominous military situation had been established, and this development was causing a great deal of alarm. It also, I went on, posed a political threat to West Germany. The issue was not whether one or another German city was to be wiped out. We eventually returned to our discussion about art, and when we parted we had reconciled, as always.

7 · OUR COMMON PAST
CATCHES UP WITH US

Ever since my first visit to Moscow in December 1969 I had been haunted by my war days in Russia; my memories actually took on a strange life of their own. I had spent over three years in the so-called Russian Campaign and had been wounded four times— when barely twenty years old. Without realizing it I was permanently marked by the tremendous physical and mental strains of that period. Later on, when I did a hitch on the Normandy front, we were confronted with a very different adversary who was far superior to us in matériel. But in Normandy we did not have the oppressive sense of being caught in an ideological struggle, which gave a special twist to the war in Russia. That, no doubt, is why few German veterans can travel to the former Soviet battle sites without feeling their hearts pound. I know many German veterans who cannot bring themselves to visit the Soviet Union as tourists.

During the first few years of my Moscow contacts, both sides spared one another's feelings by avoiding the topic of the German invasion of the Soviet Union. But in 1972 our reticence was finally ended by a chance incident. It happened when we were discussing a steel mill that was to be built in the Kursk area by the Krupp corporation. When we sat down to dinner after a long day of negotiating, the man opposite me was a senior functionary, one of the vice chairmen of Gosplan. I had come to appreciate this institution as all-powerful because of its significance for major projects within the framework of the Five-Year Plan. I asked the man where they were planning to build this huge mill. He replied: near Kursk. (And, in fact, that was where it was eventually built.) But when I questioned him more specifically about the location, he was taken aback by my persistence. From certain details I had managed to discover that this was probably an area where I had fought twice during the war—advancing and then retreating, as it were. Both battles had been heavy, and the towns had changed hands several times. I now explained the reason for my stubborn curiosity.

My dinner companion's initial reaction was one of complete surprise, after which he lapsed into thoughtful silence. I felt I had opened up a barely healed wound. He then asked if I had a son and said he had a son of eighteen. I replied that my son was seventeen. After a brief pause he told me that as a Soviet soldier he had fought in the same place and at the same time. Then he stood up and with a solemn expression raised his glass: "Let us drink a toast and promise one another that we will do everything in our power to make sure our sons never have to go through what we had to endure in our youth."

I must confess that I was deeply moved by this unexpected episode. From then on I felt relaxed and less awkward when I talked to the Soviets about the horrors of that cruel war. Since many of the people I negotiated with, both at that time and later, were of my generation, it was only natural that we could not always sidestep our mutual experiences.

Many years later, in the spring of 1985, I first met Mikhail Gorbachev, the newly elected general secretary. He, too, instantly asked me about my wartime service in his country.

It is obvious that the war, the Great Patriotic War, has left deeper and more lasting scars in Soviet minds than in German minds. The memory of the war was and is actually cultivated by the Soviets, chiefly for two reasons. First, the enormous losses of human life (their sources say the war claimed twenty million Soviets*) and the destruction of cities and industrial facilities, which could be blamed for the slowness of reconstruction and for the persistent shortages of consumer goods. Second, the Soviets—as the official rhetoric went—had to remain vigilant in confronting the expansionist, war-mongering West, and this, in turn, necessitated and justified their enormous and expensive military machine.

The Soviet population is extremely touchy about this alleged threat of war, as I learned from an experience that has lodged firmly in my mind. Soviet television began to air a series about a possible future atomic war. The program was meant to offer practical demonstrations of how to behave in case of attack: Remain calm and disciplined, take certain protective aids and devices, and proceed to the nearest subway tunnel (the Moscow subway tunnels are huge and lie far below the surface). However, the film was so realistic that many viewers panicked, thinking their country was being attacked. A lively discussion ensued, and the series was canceled.

The name "Stalingrad" says something to young people in our country and throughout the world. It represents a turning point of World War II, when the situation began to worsen for the German military. That city, which was fateful to both Soviets and Germans, was long ago renamed Volgograd, after the river on whose banks it lies, and it has also been given the honorary title of "Heroic City." Throughout the formerly occupied countries, however, its earlier name (which the French use for a boulevard in northern Paris) still symbolizes the start of their liberation.

In 1986 when I headed the German team in our joint banking commission, I traveled to Volgograd. This city is an industrial metropolis today with many public parks and endless, virtually ruler-drawn avenues. Yet one ubiquitously comes upon places that recall the fierce fighting of the fall and winter of 1942–43.

* In May 1990, in Washington, Gorbachev set the total at 27 million dead. But it is unclear whether this figure refers to combat casualties exclusively.

Our delegation was given a solemn and impressive welcome by the district chairman and the city fathers, and I was presented with a memento of my visit—a miniature of Mother Russia. This huge statue of a woman brandishing a sword stands in the northern part of the city on the once hotly contested peak of Mamai Kurgan. She dominates the flat, steppelike landscape around the lower reaches of the Volga.

We were then told that the Soviet delegation would be going to the memorial for the heroes of the Red Army in order to lay a wreath. My Soviet co-chairman was in the Moscow cabinet, and I learned that according to an official decree any member of the government who visits a Heroic City is required to attend an appropriate ceremony. When I heard about this ritual, I told my hosts that the German team would be accompanying the Soviets at a respectful distance. I would, I said, appreciate their allowing us to commemorate the German soldiers who had died in this area.

The Soviets were taken aback at first. Our representative from the German embassy in Moscow whispered to me that such a request had never before been made here, nor had it been cleared with the Foreign Office in Bonn. I replied that I was not a government official, I was head of a German banking delegation, and besides, as a war veteran I felt that such a request was appropriate. I made a similar statement to the Soviets. All of us, I added, Germans and Soviets, had spent several days negotiating, and every morning the Soviets had emphasized how important our work was in terms of improving relations and ensuring peace. Stalingrad, in particular, was a tragic symbol of the sufferings that Russians and Germans had inflicted on each other. That, I said, was why, in this very city, we needed conciliatory gestures such as I had taken the liberty of proposing.

After a bit of conferring and pondering, the Soviets decided to respect my request, and so our German team participated in the solemn laying of the wreath. Soviet passersby were watching the ceremony. The monument to the heroes stood in a small park not far from where General Field Marshal Friedrich Paulus, commander in chief of the besieged Sixth German Army, had set up his final headquarters in the ruins of a department store. In order to bolster Paulus's morale, Hitler had promoted him to marshal in late July 1943, but Paulus soon surrendered anyway. I was shown the sign on the street where the department store had once stood: Peace Street. The change was not recent; the street had been renamed back in 1944 before the war even ended.

After laying the wreath at the monument, we went over to Mamai Kurgan where we slowly and solemnly climbed the steps, over soil that mercifully covers the mangled remains of warriors on both sides. The hilltop is crowned with a rotunda on whose walls are engraved in gold letters the names of thousands of Soviet soldiers who died here. At the center of the rotunda, a gigantic fist clutches an eternal torch. Visitors, who are obviously moved, usually form a procession and slowly mount the spiral steps, accompanied by solemn music. On that day I was told that the music we heard, Schumann's *Träumerei*, had been chosen as a gesture of reconciliation.

Volgograd has a war museum. In its vast, partly subterranean facilities, it exhibits detailed depictions of the battle with original weapons and equipment belonging to both armies. There is no trace of polemics in the commentaries of the supervisory staff. For Soviet and perhaps also German visitors, Volgograd can serve as a warning and as a caution against an all-too-willing desire to forget.

Another incident reminded me of the dreadful days of the war. In February 1987, General Secretary Gorbachev organized the so-called Moscow Peace Conference (which I plan to discuss below). On this occasion Mr. Alkhimov, the head of Soviet banking and a recipient of the Hero of the Soviet Union gold-star medal, the highest Soviet award equivalent to the American Medal of Honor, asked me whether I could get him a description of old Königsberg, a formerly German and now Soviet city that has been renamed Kaliningrad. I asked him why Königsberg of all

places, and he replied that he had fought there in the spring of
1945 and had taken part in its capture. Now it was my turn to
gape because I had likewise fought there that same winter and
spring. From the other side of the Pregel River my outfit had
watched the final, merciless battle for the tormented city, which
fell in April 1945. The hinterland, called Samland, was not occupied until later. Now the highly decorated former Soviet officer
was sitting next to the former German officer. By 1987 we already
had more than ten years of cooperation and mutual respect behind us, and now that dreadful past flashed into our present.

It was indeed bizarre. The war in Russia had two human aspects
for us Germans—I don't know how else to describe it. The man
I was facing, Alkhimov, was a representative of the Red Army. In
the grips of ideology, we had fought those men ruthlessly, and
they, too, had shown us no quarter. But as hostile invaders in
their country we inevitably got to know the people even as we
confiscated their property, their villages and cottages. There are
many stories to tell, but I will limit myself to a single incident,
the memory of which is still fresh in my mind.

The premature and unusually harsh winter of 1941–42 has
often been described as the natural phenomenon that caused the
German offensive to bog down at the outskirts of Moscow. The
weather certainly brought difficulties and surprises for which we
were totally unprepared. With temperatures plunging to fifty
degrees and more below zero and icy east winds blasting across
the flat, snow-covered reaches, sheer survival was more important
than huge military operations. The barest physical needs, especially warmth, had top priority. The only way soldiers in the field
could escape the elements was to find shelter in the wretched
shacks of the local peasants.

These shacks, which were usually built of clay, were winter-
ized in the fall and had small double-paned, if not triple-paned
storm windows to keep the wind at bay as much as possible. The
cracks were stuffed with strips of *Pravda* newsprint, and wood
and dried cowpats were stored under the stove. The entire family,

from grandmother to baby, along with the small livestock such as chickens and pigs, made themselves comfortable on top of or beneath the huge stove. This whitewashed stove filled most of the shack, which was literally built around it. The people put on whatever clothes they had and girded themselves for months of living like this.

We adjusted to the routine in this crowded space—conditions that were bound to bring us closer together. We shared the most basic necessities, often giving away part of our rations even though we could not always count on additional supplies. The women did our laundry and helped us in the fight against lice, which were feared as typhus carriers. The highly effective weapons the women deployed against the lice were oversized irons that were heated in the oven.

Alarms were sounded repeatedly, forcing us to charge out into the cold and defend outselves against the attacking Russians. During those winter months we often fought against marvelously trained Siberians who, dressed in winter camouflage, silently approached us on their skis. No sooner had we beaten them off than we scurried back into the warm shacks of our "quartermasters."

At that time the full absurdity of this war dawned on me. We were enjoying some tender loving care from a Russian peasant woman when all at once we tore ourselves from her stove, dashed outdoors, and began shooting at her compatriots, perhaps her sons! This schizoid situation caused me, a lieutenant of only nineteen, a tremendous amount of turmoil. I still feel profound respect today for the simple, pious Russian peasant woman.

8 · A FEW COMMENTS ABOUT
THE COUNTRY AND
THE PEOPLE

During my first few visits to Moscow in the winter 1969–70, I was struck by how different life seemed here compared with life in other world capitals. In those days there were almost no private cars to be seen here. The passengers in the countless black government limousines were usually functionaries. The rank and file had the standard model, a Moskvich; higher echelons were assigned Volgas; and VIPs were honored with roomy six- to eight-seat Chaikas. The Chaika, with its lavish use of chrome, was modeled after huge American luxury limousines of the 1950s. On many mornings these majestic "state coaches" could be spotted at the gates of the Kremlin. Later on they were replaced by a new version that mimicked the American Lincoln.

Eventually I was promoted to "guest of the state." This meant that I was driven in Chaikas, sometimes even with a flashing blue light and an escort car. I was accorded these privileges even in distant Soviet republics such as Armenia, Georgia, Azerbaijan, and Uzbekistan. Comfortable as these posh rides were in the capital or the provinces, the circumstances could be unpleasant, even embarrassing, for a foreign guest. Pedestrians would scoot out of the way the instant a Chaika heaved into view. On highways and byways the escort car with the blue police light made sure that all the oncoming vehicles—trucks, passenger cars, horse-drawn wagons—squeezed over to the right side of the road and waited until the convoy had passed. If anyone hesitated for even an instant, the police gruffly interrogated him or took down his name.

My preferential treatment made me uneasy, and I tried to compensate by looking as friendly as I could or waving at the people who were respectfully biding their time. But I soon realized that they were puzzled by my gesture. For decades now, since czarist days and the revolutionary government, privileges for the elite are taken for granted here and endured without protest.

The chauffeurs of these road hogs for the privileged are usually ruthless in exercising their right of way, which makes the increasingly denser traffic more and more dangerous. The Muscovites have a saying: If you cross at the green, you risk being hit by a car. If you use the pedestrian crossing, you have a right to be hit.

Allow me to digress briefly. During my numerous stays in Moscow and my travels through the Soviet Union, the officials always offered me exemplary hospitality from my arrival to my departure. This was especially true whenever my family came along. From time to time not just my wife but also my son and my daughter wanted to observe what I was doing on my frequent trips to this enigmatic country on which I often heaped negative and reproachful comments. My family wasn't just curious, they wanted to express a kind of solidarity with me in a situation that was not always easy. Their pleasure was dimmed, of course, whenever they watched officials bullying, even harassing, the nonprivileged.

At times my family actually wanted me to go to the Soviet Union as frequently as possible. Those were the years after 1977 when terrorists cruelly assassinated leading public figures in West Germany. Since I, too, was a potential target, I had to follow the security instructions of our Criminal Investigation Bureau, which meant that I could enjoy relative freedom of movement only when traveling abroad. Foreign guests and businessmen were astounded by the sight of armed sentries guarding my office entrance.

Victor Ivanov, the Soviet deputy minister of foreign trade, was unable to conceal his surprise. With a touch of cynicism he said that if these guards were necessary, then I'd be better off in Moscow. He added that during my many visits to his country I must have realized I could move about in complete safety. Objectively, he was right. But I also knew the price one had to pay for this security—an oppressive police state that smothered the very seeds of crime or terrorism before they could sprout and, more important, subdued virtually all desires for individual liberty.

But back to the Muscovites. Moscow was and still is a city of pedestrians. Granted, the number of private cars has grown visibly (I'm told that the new ones belong primarily to waiters in restaurants open only to foreigners, where bills are paid chiefly in hard Western currency). But despite the increase in vehicular traffic, Moscow's street scene is dominated by the columns of pedestrians hurrying along the wide sidewalks. Most of these heavily laden people are charging toward the subway stations. The tableau was the same twenty years ago, but in that winter it looked infinitely bleak. Against the dirty, grayish white background of a snowy metropolis, thousands of wraithlike creatures were marching along practically in lockstep. Hushed, gloomy, and all in black, they looked like a funeral procession. During the past two decades things have gradually brightened up—quite literally.

I will never forget a millinery shop on Gorky Prospekt, a huge boulevard. Amid the drab and dull displays in the other stores, this window stood out because of its elaborate lighting. Women's hats were meticulously arranged—now higher, now lower, and somehow unreal—in a poignant effort to catch the eye of the indifferent pedestrians who were hurrying past.

The once uniformly dismal sight of the clothing—even that of the young people in Moscow—livened up bit by bit. I knew that

Russian women liked to sew and had a knack for it. In the early seventies when we moved into our first offices at the Hotel Metropol, we were lucky to have the services of a capable Russian-speaking secretary from our home office. We were permitted to bring her to Moscow as a German employee on a temporary basis. In those days getting such permission was extremely difficult. Our "show lady" was not only capable but also good-looking. She usually wore a chic denim suit. Back then, blue jeans were all the rage, and a woman's denim suit was an absolute sensation. Russian women who spotted our secretary instantly made sketches of her attractive ensemble in order to reproduce it at home.

During the seventies the first tourists to crop up in Moscow stayed at either the Intourist or the Rossiya. For a long time the Rossiya, with its four thousand beds, was the largest hotel in the capital. For the local women who were curious about Western fashions, the hotel offered a large amount of visual instruction to give them new ideas. As a result, even though the Russians were rigidly isolated from foreigners, the Moscow street scene took on more and more Western touches, which made it a friendlier city. Several years ago the Soviets had a brainstorm, and their shops began carrying dress patterns produced by a German firm so that Russian women could make their own fashionable clothing. A small expenditure of hard currency proved to be a highly successful investment. In the old days I used to bring along pantyhose as gifts for women, but today the dress patterns are greatly in demand.

It was not just the clothing, however; their overall behavior started to change during the mid-seventies. The young people in particular struck me as more relaxed and self-confident. All at once young women began wearing the miniskirt, which by now was passé in the West but still officially taboo in the Soviet Union. I found it surprising that suddenly they were putting more emphasis on makeup. I saw eyeliner being used for the first time, and lipstick was applied more frequently and more seductively. Our three Russian secretaries, who were pretty and charming (albeit checked and continually double-checked by the KGB), proved to be true fashion pioneers.

I have to add an observation I made during my first trip to the hermetically sealed empire. This experience might trigger a smile rather than serious pondering. During the early seventies when a sojourn in Moscow was not exactly a pleasure junket, we were nevertheless curious to find out all about the peculiarities of the Soviet system and life-style. One evening I met a Western visitor at the Hotel National, who was familiar with Moscow. He suggested that I stay on a bit longer than usual at the bar for foreigners (who paid in foreign currency) and promised I would be surprised. The place was filled with men, but shortly before midnight several very pretty young women walked in. Their clothes and makeup were elegant, which was quite unusual in those days. During this period when the Soviets were closely shielded from the West, we had been warned that this was a land of pristine morals, to which capitalist decadence had no access. But lo and behold, these pert ladies did not play hard to get. Through the billows of cigar and cigarette smoke I saw one woman after another vanishing with a client. What I couldn't find out, however, was where they actually went. If you were staying at the hotel, you could enter your room only after being thoroughly checked by the female hall supervisor who guarded the keys. Taxis were practically nonexistent. And we all knew that private apartments afforded little privacy. Some other arrangement must have been made. At any rate, when I met with the Soviets the next morning, I couldn't help pointing out that some highly reprehensible Western customs had already gained a foothold in their clean, puritanical system. They were visibly embarrassed.

Any description of the Russians must include their powerful religious ties, which have helped to mold their character. Marx, as we know, called religion the opium of the people, thereby summing up the basic thesis of the atheist state. When I was a soldier in Russia, I kept looking for signs of this aggressive atheism, but I discovered the very opposite. In towns and villages the churches of a bygone era had been transformed into warehouses or meeting halls for the Communist Party. But far from the large settlements, almost every clay cottage had something like a prayer nook in its single room or in its parlor. This nook usually contained a small icon depicting the Virgin; although naively simple, it was usually painted with profound devotion. The tiny lamp in front of the icon had gone without oil or wax for a long time now, but it at least sported a withered twig or a bunch of dried wild flowers. I would often watch the peasants, usually the older ones, furtively crossing themselves three times in the Orthodox style and bowing to the icon.

Once, to my surprise, I stumbled upon services in a neglected, dilapidated church. This was my first experience with the rites of the Eastern church. The sonorous chant of the deacon and the ardor of the worshipers were both impressive and baffling. I concluded that despite a quarter century of atheistic policies, there were still traces of active religious ties among the people.

When I returned to the Soviet Union many years later, those earlier scenes were still sharply etched in my mind, and I noted that my wartime observations remained valid. I am tempted to say that transcendency is inherent in the Russian soul.

We are constantly reminded of this quality by the Russian literature known in the West—Pushkin, Dostoevsky, Tolstoy, Chekhov, Pasternak, Solzhenitzyn. Even the most brutal attempts to eradicate this "superstition" have failed. At times the regime tried to created a surrogate religion in the Lenin and Stalin cult. When the Stalin cult began crumbling under Brezhnev, the government did its best to use Marxism and Leninism as articles of faith. It seems that only the year 1988, when Russians celebrated the millennium of their conversion to Christianity, brought about a change.

But let us discuss Dostoevsky for a moment. As a man of both deep faith and skepticism, he, like few others, suffered through what he himself called a "great purgatory." Critics often describe his Orthodox piety as "mystical"—an adjective that recurs throughout Russian literature of the nineteenth century and is applied to Russian art even today. Dostoevsky's faith was obviously a doubter's faith. Nevertheless, he felt that the Russian people had the mission of being the "bearer of God":

> The calling of all Russia is Orthodoxy, the light from the East—a light that shall flow toward the people of the West, the people who have lost Christ.

This is an almost nationalistic Russian-Slavic messianism that took aim at the so-called Westerners during the second half of the nineteenth century. They were accused of having lost Christ—a reproach hurled at the ideas of the Enlightenment, at liberalism, atheism, materialism, and socialism (for Dostoevsky, synonymous with communism), and at the increasing German influence on Russian politics. This went on until the early years of our century.

Grand Duke Vladimir of Kiev, after examining the suitability of all other religions, ordered his people to adopt the Orthodox faith as the one and only redeeming religion. In 1988 when the Russian Orthodox Church was preparing to celebrate its thousandth anniversary, the question was often asked: Why did Vladimir's people accept this high-handed edict so quickly and then preserve this religion so fervently through all sorts of catastrophes and confusions? Dostoevsky provides an explanation that helps us understand Russian Orthodoxy. He opens our eyes to a typical feature of the Russian soul—the "intrinsic spiritual need to suffer": "Russians," he writes, "have always had this craving for suffering."

This trait is probably also due to Russia's geography and early history. Prior to its subsequent conquests, ancient Russia had a flat terrain that lay wide open, unprotected, and vulnerable to any solid enemy attack. Aside from the rivers flowing north to south, Russia had no natural obstacles that could have been developed for defense purposes. Its highest point was just thirteen hundred feet above sea level. Tartars, Kalmucks, and Mongols: Their mounted hordes easily conquered this land. Its vastness and climate did not become its natural allies until the second round—a lesson learned with such dire results by Napoleon's grand army and by German troops in two world wars.

Because of these historical experiences—the great sufferings inflicted by foreign invasions and the oppression of foreign rule—the Russians learned to appreciate Christ's passion as "an example and a solace." For the Russians the glorious resurrection of the Son of God is full of the most wonderful promise. At Easter they greet one another by saying: "Christ has risen!" We Germans celebrate Christmas, the birth of Christ, as the major holiday when we exchange presents and good wishes, but for the Russians, Easter is the most sublime event of the year. If you have had the good fortune to experience the Russian celebration of Easter, you will never forget that profound feeling of natural, almost naive religious faith.

Orthodox Christianity has made a stronger and more lasting impact on Russia than is apparent at first glance. When the new faith was decreed a thousand years ago, the Russians set out on a special path. The Mongolian tyranny then isolated the Russians almost entirely from the West (except for Novgorod, which was a member of the Hanseatic League). For that reason alone, the development of the Russians differed from that of the rest of Europe; they were involved only peripherally in the history of the West.

The Russian orientation toward Constantinople as a religious hub led to a rigid hierarchy that prescribed not only the overall caste structure but also the individual's role within the society. Nevertheless, the Russian Orthodox Church, which was even tolerated by the Mongols (as long as taxes were paid on time), was the only institution that allowed the populace to maintain its own identity vis-à-vis the Golden Horde as well as the Poles and Lithuanians. For generations one of the most urgent concerns of the Russians was to avoid total surrender despite spiritual and economic decline and political disintegration. According to Dostoevsky:

> The school of Christianity, which the nation attended, consisted of centuries of countless sufferings and afflictions, as recorded in its history. Those were centuries in which the nation was abandoned and trampled by everyone while forced to labor for all and sundry.

And it was the Church that created a new power center in the early fourteenth century; it did so—with the duke's permission—by moving the seat of the capital from Kiev to Vladimir Susdal and then to Moscow. Ivan I could begin "gathering the Russian soil." Ivan III had himself anointed "czar of all the Russias"; next, after marrying the niece of the last Byzantine emperor, he declared Moscow the bulwark of Orthodoxy and the Third Rome. In 1492 the czar, with the Church's blessing, launched a series of virtually endless wars against the (Catholic) Lithuanians and Poles. Those wars have never been forgotten on either side of the border. From then on, spiritual and secular power could no longer be separated. They supported (or fought) one another in order to strengthen their own positions, increase their wealth, and keep the people in line.

Thus, Russia was absorbed in its domestic affairs while Western Europe developed the foundations of the modern world. In Russia the reverberations of the Renaissance, with its epoch-making knowledge, were felt only at the ducal courts—and then like distant echoes. Nevertheless, the fusion of Western and Byzantine elements led to marvelous achievements, especially in architecture. Just ponder the churches of the Kremlin or the monasteries in and around Moscow.

The Enlightenment, ultimately climaxing in the French Revolution, guided the minds of Central and Western Europe into new channels but completely bypassed Eastern Europe. The concepts of democracy and a constitutional state had only a minor impact on Russia's development. Philosophers such as Kant, Hegel, and Schiller were certainly read here and are still honored today, but they have influenced only a relatively tiny number of intellectuals. Needless to say, this only served to widen the gap between aristocracy, intelligentsia, and the masses.

Peter the Great single-mindedly opened up his country to Western European science and technology, but he could make little headway in his gigantic effort to free Russia from the fetters of its backwardness and isolation. Czar Alexander's attempts at forging a constitution were likewise resolutely undermined. The Bolshevik revolution brought new isolation from Central and Western Europe. It was only after Brezhnev that a lasting change commenced.

However, seventy years of Soviet rule have failed to eliminate the rifts and contradictions in state and society. Old Russia, with its Orthodox Church and its historical and spiritual tradition, is emerging from under the veneer of progress and atheism. The ideology of the revolution was able to mobilize those people who were no longer spiritually bound to the Church. But today the Russians feel that the political system has outlived its usefulness; it is no longer worth fighting for. In the era of glasnost and perestroika, latent tensions are again erupting in the form of ethnic, social, and economic crises.

To sum it all up: On the one side we have the great achievements in creating a modern, industrialized Soviet Union; on the other side, the daily encounter with ancient forces (especially in the non-European part). The communist rulers in the Kremlin tried to link and blend certain elements of the Eurasian continent, but those elements have never really joined together; they are still worlds apart.

The reform movement in the Soviet Union demands a social reorientation and individual perspectives of development. Moscow is discussing models for autonomy that would take into account the intrinsic cultural features of more than a hundred Soviet nationalities. They are looking chiefly to the West for examples. After centuries of being cordoned off from the rest of Europe, however, the Soviets may not always be able to apply the categories of the Western tradition, which in its broadest sense also includes America. Nonetheless, the restructuring of Soviet society cannot be done without the traditional forces. Among those elements that have not been destroyed by the system, the Orthodox Church is at the top of the list, for it is deeply rooted in the populace while its opposition has only recently moved beyond a relatively small group of intellectuals. Russians, White Russians, and Ukrainians simply have a "Christian" heritage in the broadest sense of the term, and this makes them bearers of the European cultural legacy.

At this point we have to consider an issue that is only now being thrashed out in the Soviet Union. The official Orthodox Church compromised itself when, following the tradition of czarist times, it made its peace with the Soviet government, even supporting it at certain phases. Religion had to be shaped differently in order to survive within the very narrow pale of government tolerance. This means that having lost some credibility among the people, the Orthodox Church will now have to pursue its own brand of perestroika.

I had my reasons for mentioning Boris Pasternak in my description of the Russian mentality and religious faith. In 1958 Pasternak was awarded the Nobel Prize for his novel *Doctor Zhivago,* but he was not allowed to accept it. He died four years later after being persecuted in his homeland and officially proscribed. He was idolized by the younger Soviet generation, however, and greatly admired in the West. Pasternak lies buried in Peredelkino, a picturesque village near Moscow. In 1972 when I attempted to visit his grave, I still had a vivid picture of how shamefully the dying writer had been treated by the Moscow functionaries. Visits to his grave were not officially permitted, and Pasternak's charisma was evidently still so powerful that the functionaries hoped to force him into oblivion. But as we know today, they failed.

Back then, in 1972, I finally arrived at the small cemetery in

Peredelkino, where I found Pasternak's grave in a dense grove of birches. I noticed a middle-aged man and a young woman who were busy making benches out of rough birch branches. I could tell they were not cemetery employees. My heart began to pound because I was walking along a forbidden path. We began to converse, and it turned out that the man was a lecturer at the University of Moscow and the woman was his assistant. The Russians have the lovely custom of placing benches around graves so that friends and relatives of the deceased can sit down and chat with him or with others about him. I learned this from these two people who spoke to me in an open and friendly way. This pleasant encounter made a lasting impression on me.

Sixteen years later, in the fall of 1988, I again felt an urge to visit the great writer's grave. A small headstone had long since been placed there; it showed his profile and the dates of his birth and death. The site had been turned into a small family tomb: His wife was buried on one side, his son on the other. Apples, ears of corn, and bits of cake were lying on Pasternak's grave. I was told that such provisions for a journey are left as love offerings on the grave of a venerated person. What bothered me, however, was that the visitors had evidently honored only the writer, not his wife and son.

My companions and I sat down on the rough wooden bench and lapsed into silence. We were immersed in reflection on this sunny autumn afternoon when we were joined by a simple man holding a plastic bag. At first he, too, remained silent, then he said softly, almost to himself: "We miss Pasternak. He left us much too early." Peering at our obviously Western European urban clothes, he asked where we were from. He was startled to hear that we were Germans, from West Germany. Eventually he said: "Then you are our enemies. I was a partisan, I fought the invading Germans near Gomel."

"And I was stationed there as a German soldier," I murmured.

Our minds dwelled on this brief graveside dialogue as we sat on the small, crowded bench, each of us absorbed in his own thoughts. We were later joined by two young men. One was a student, the other had been a student at the time of Pasternak's death. He told us that in those days there had been a government blackout on all information about Pasternak's health, but illegal leaflets had kept the students up to date. That was how they learned of his death, despite the strictest official secrecy. Unfortunately, a huge contingent of militiamen had prevented any attendance at the funeral.

It was common knowledge that Pasternak had picked out the grave site long before his death. It was located in the small cemetery, which the writer saw from his dacha on a nearby hill, and marked by a towering tree. For many years no one was allowed to visit his grave. Supposedly the government even installed microphones in the adjacent trees to record the conversations of visitors. This rumor can't be verified, of course, but considering how the government acted when Pasternak died, such snooping seems quite possible.

9 · ISOLATION, VERTICAL THINKING, AND IMMOBILISM

In late 1979 when Soviet troops marched into Afghanistan, the preparations for the Moscow Summer Olympics were under way. All the essential preliminary preparation had been taken care of. The overall organizing, which could be handled only by a gigantic, centrally ruled state, had been determined down to the last detail. The worldwide promotional campaigns for the Festival of Peace had been launched long ago. For quite a while now all our talks with the Soviets, whether in Moscow or in West Germany, had centered on the topic of the 1980 Olympiad. Now, the Soviets exerted strenuous efforts to overcome the negative image created by their invasion.

But then came the blow that sent them reeling: The United States canceled its participation in the games. Then, in May 1980, the West German Olympic Committee joined the boycott. The Soviets were distressed and virtually panicked. With completely exaggerated notions of my power, a Soviet delegation headed for Düsseldorf to coax me into intervening. I assured them that this matter fell outside my jurisdiction, but they refused to believe me. After years of dealing with them, I was familiar with these officials, and now they were begging me to do everything in my power to avoid jeopardizing our joint efforts toward greater understanding. I tried to explain the issue, but they thought I was rationalizing. Thoroughly disappointed, the delegation finally returned home.

Such misunderstandings of facts were typical of Soviet officials. I was unable to make them realize which points I was authorized to negotiate and which were absolutely beyond my mandate. During the years of tension, when Moscow and Bonn were cold-shouldering each other, the Soviets still saw me on a regular basis. They would seize every opportunity to voice their criticism of Bonn's policies in general and its actions in particular. Often they were merely venting their anger on me.

As a result our meetings were sometimes limited to vague outlines. Naturally, I kept Bonn abreast of our talks—which the Soviets understood, of course. Once when I told Hans-Dietrich Genscher, our foreign minister, that I felt uneasy about this practice, he said tersely: "We're not on speaking terms. If you see any chance of conversation, grab it. The main thing is to keep talking."

Well, my field wasn't politics, it was trade relations between our two countries. Earlier, our commerce with the Soviet Union had been minimal compared to our commerce with Western nations. This low percentage had more of a political than a truly economic meaning. The Soviets were intent on nurturing contacts with the West through foreign trade. But in 1973–74 this emphasis shifted with the start of the oil crisis. Suddenly, by exporting oil and gas, Moscow was acquiring huge amounts of Western currency, which constituted up to eighty percent of its total export proceeds.

Like a spider in its web, the Foreign Trade Ministry (now Foreign Economic Ministry) directed and controlled all of Moscow's links with other countries. For many years this ministry was headed by Nikolai Patolichev, whom I have already mentioned. As an old-guard Communist he had great influence in the government. In our negotiations he represented the political side, as it were, even though our negotiating partner was actually Deputy Minister Victor Ivanov, a highly knowledgeable and down-to-earth expert. During the seventies we were joined by Yuri Brezhnev; this son of the general secretary of the Communist Party was the first deputy minister for foreign trade. In the Soviet hierarchy, each minister has several deputies, their number depending on the importance of his specific ministry. We had grown accustomed to recognizing a first deputy minister as the "real" minister.

I met Brezhnev's son a number of times. He never struck me as having any real expertise in his field, but then, I never had a chance to put him to the test. The Soviet functionaries always acted somewhat reserved toward him or mildly friendly. As far as I could judge he never played a vital role. From our conversations I had the impression that he felt out of his element. He obviously enjoyed the distractions of Western nightlife, but he was not alone in this respect. At any rate, Yuri Brezhnev was given a somewhat special treatment by the Western firms negotiating with the Soviets. At times I wished that some well-meaning friend would advise Brezhnev, Sr., to leave his son at home. Nevertheless, I got along with the son and fully sympathized with his unfortunate position.

My real problem was the centralized planning and the gap between the Moscow ministries and the provinces. I always felt I was running up against stone walls. Nikolai Tikhonov (who eventually became premier) once asked me how we could increase trade between our two countries. I made the following suggestion: Check directly with the leader of a regional government or the chief of a collective combine somewhere in this enormous Soviet domain and ask him directly what his needs are, then encourage him to talk to the directors of West German firms and decide which exports would be most useful to both sides. But Tikhonov gruffly retorted that this was not workable. Everything had to go through Moscow, that is, the Foreign Trade Ministry. It would take years, I thought to myself, to gradually eliminate this Moscow bottleneck. Today, decentralized negotiating is actually encouraged in the Soviet Union, although none of us has ever practiced it and negotiators have no experience to fall back on.

For years now, agriculture has been the number-one Soviet headache. Foreign countries, especially the United States and Italy, have given assistance by providing machines and know-how. In West Germany numerous small and medium-sized companies have volunteered their assistance but gotten nowhere—mainly due to a lack of concerted action on the Soviet side.

Then I started negotiating with Deputy Premier Z. N. Nuriyev, the Soviet coordinator of agricultural affairs. In 1983 when our talks began, General Secretary Yuri Andropov's regime seemed more open-minded than that of his predecessor Brezhnev. Drowsy, vegetating functionaries were suddenly transformed into committed, thinking, responsible officials to whom one could talk and who knew how to listen.

Nuriyev, my negotiating counterpart, stated honestly that the situation really was deplorable. He pointed out that only a fraction of the last, rich potato harvest had reached consumers. At fault were mundane transportation difficulties. Most of the population lives in the western part of the gigantic country, but most of the industrial raw materials are in the north and the east, and most of the food in the south. Consequently, resources and consumer centers lie thousands of miles apart. Until the 1980s, for example, the Soviets had no network of refrigerated trucks and/or freight cars to supply consumers with high-quality perishables—say, produce from farming areas in Uzbekistan, Moldavia, Georgia, Armenia, or Crimea.

Mr. Nuriyev and I quickly came to terms. We agreed on how we—that is, the bank—would proceed in providing advice and establishing contacts with the appropriate firms. In the agricultural department, Mr. Nuriyev was in charge of eleven subministries, each with a special function such as livestock, fruits and vegetables, grains, and so forth. In swapping experiences with these subministries, I stumbled on yet another calamitous situation, which I have already mentioned. What turned out to be the greatest obstacle to any productive cooperation was the worst kind of departmentalized thinking.

The number of subministries was legion. I have never been able to pinpoint the exact figure mainly because it keeps changing; there are probably more than a hundred. Each such department is assigned a specific area and has no contact with neighboring departments. I have already described the resulting tunnel vision. Opinions and experiences are never exchanged, and the flow of communication is strictly vertical. The various departments know little about one another, and this mutual insulation—indeed, obstruction of horizontal contacts—is exacerbated by the failure to move funds between departments. Whenever a department takes in Western currency for its profitable exports, the proceeds remain within that department and can only be used there instead of benefiting other departments that might be in need of money. As I frequently observed, a department might be prevented from carrying out a certain task for lack of Western currency to buy equipment available only in the West. As a result, a department's capacity was untapped or at best underutilized. Similar cases of underachievement occur when it comes to acquiring an expensive machine that may not be cost effective in one plant but could be worth the price if it were shared by several plants. This would require teamwork among multiple departments or factories, but for the reasons I have gone into, such cooperation is not yet possible.

In Bonn's ministries, too, departmental thinking and interdepartmental rivalries can sometimes interfere with cooperation, but in the Soviet system a department is rigidly bound to an assigned area and the staff has been trained to focus purely on implementing a specific plan—and that's all. They never think in terms of the integral totality or coordinated procedures.

In the fall of 1983, Andropov lost much of his clout because of his critical illness, and the first timid efforts at reform and individual initiative yielded to the kind of lethargy we had witnessed for fourteen years. When Andropov was succeeded by

Konstantin Chernenko, who was likewise ill and visibly aging, all initiative vanished among the Soviets. It was hopeless even to think of changing the existing conditions. Immobilism—the tendency to avoid risk—regained the upper hand.

Try as we might, we got nowhere with our agricultural consulting initiative. Finally I asked who at the politburo was in charge of agriculture. The answer: Talk to Mikhail Gorbachev, who was described as a young, dynamic functionary. I tried to arrange a meeting with him in 1984, but even though I was promised an appointment, it never came through. As they informed me, however, he knew about our suggestions and had received the necessary documents. I was told to plan for a meeting with him in early 1985.

We were very curious about Gorbachev. Was he simply one more link in the endless chain of apparatchiks to whose conduct and mentality we had slowly grown accustomed? Or could he be a reformer of Andropov's stamp, a man who would fling the windows open again? Nevertheless, by the beginning of 1985 the Soviets whom we knew rather well told us very privately that Gorbachev was the man to keep an eye on. His name was also cropping up in Western newspapers. In the fall of 1984, during his tenure at the politburo, Gorbachev had visited British Prime Minister Margaret Thatcher. His astounding frankness caused quite a stir.

10·A NEW MAN AND
A FRESH WIND

In March 1985, Mikhail Gorbachev was chosen to succeed Chernenko as general secretary of the Soviet Communist Party. I was scheduled to visit Moscow in mid-April of that year. Shortly before my departure I was notified that the new general secretary wanted to see me on April 18. Eventually it turned out that this was one of his first talks ever with a foreigner, and in his new capacity this was his first meeting with a representative of a Western country.

How puzzling. Why did he wish to speak with me of all people—an officer of a major capitalist bank? In the course of our meeting, which lasted two hours longer than planned, it became obvious that Gorbachev wanted to converse informally, without adhering to an agenda or struggling with protocol. It quickly dawned on me that the new master of the Kremlin was discarding the old and rigid rules of conduct, with their stodgy patterns and often boring rehashes of long-familiar positions.

I had already noticed this change when we drove through the gates of the Kremlin. Next to me sat my mentor, Vladimir Alkhimov, who as president of Gosbank was in charge of the entire Soviet banking system. He told me that he wasn't quite sure what we would be talking about, no list of topics had been prepared. Gorbachev, he said, wanted to have a general conversation that was not limited to specific issues. The important thing, Alkhimov added, was that I be candid in my answers.

This preamble, which had probably been discussed by the two men, was in itself unusual. For all my previous meetings with high-ranking Soviet functionaries, the topics had always been meticulously mapped out in advance. Occasionally certain items that I was very interested in were if not crossed out then at least disqualified with the words: "To be avoided as far as possible." This time, however, no such precautions had been observed.

We were taken to the Kremlin's administrative wing where Gorbachev's office was located. For years now I had been familiar with these long corridors, all of which sported identical runners. The arrangements are the same throughout the various administrative wings, even the one that can be entered only with special permission. This wing, incidentally, also contained Lenin's office and his modest apartment, in which nothing has been changed. Today those rooms are maintained as a museum that one can view after acquiring a special permit.

When Gorbachev asked us into his office, the first thing I noticed was the smell of fresh paint. These quarters had obviously been spruced up shortly before the new tenant moved in. Through the windows, which were half covered with starched white curtains, I could make out Red Square beyond Lenin's tomb. The general secretary was waiting for me in the center of the room, with the secretary of the politburo at his side. Completely relaxed, Gorbachev came toward me, greeting me with an open and friendly face. He remarked that I must be familiar with his country since I had seen action here as a soldier. He then mentioned several place names—the sites of battles in which I had fought. Gorbachev also spoke about the great tank battle of Kharkov; but I had to break in and correct him: I had participated in the battle of Kursk. I was not surprised at his detailed knowledge of my background; after all, I had been involved in not exactly unimportant negotiations with Moscow for fifteen years now. I took it for granted that the Soviets had compiled a detailed dossier on me.

Our subsequent dialogue was so unusual, so utterly different from all my earlier conversations with the Soviets that I would also like to describe the atmosphere. Gorbachev never once took his eyes off me. His expression was both likable and compelling, and everything he said revealed great intelligence combined with a fascinating analytic skill. His questions, eschewing empty rhetoric, were blunt and to the point, and his answers precise and thorough.

Gorbachev opened our discussion with a brief historical and philosophical preface. He said that the era of ideological animosity was over: "We're not living in the age of medieval crusaders." Even though we had gone through hard times, he went on, our two nations—Soviets and Germans—had not grown apart irrevocably. Our goal was now to improve the economic and political relations between our countries. To avoid a new disaster we had to learn from the past and never forget it. He praised Willy Brandt, whose friendship treaties with Moscow and Warsaw showed that he had learned from history. When Gorbachev touched upon Chancellor Helmut Kohl, he anxiously asked me where West Germany was heading. I replied: "Our federal government, like its predecessors, will adhere to the spirit and the letter of our treaties. It is fully aware of the importance of its political relations with the East European states."

Gorbachev dug in his heels: "Missiles are stationed on the soil of the Federal Republic of Germany. They perceptibly worsen the overall situation. Europe ought to get rid of these nuclear weapons. The United States wants Europe to bear the brunt of anything aimed at America. Evidently the United States also wants to have a means of pressuring Europe and the Soviet Union even in peacetime. What use is that to the European governments? Cultural and economic exchange could do a lot more good. After all, Europe is the cradle of civilization."

I replied, "We have been told by military experts that you, the Soviets, have installed more than 420 SS-20 missiles, which comes to more than twelve hundred warheads, some of which are pointed at Western Europe. They constitute an immediate threat for us. West Germany has no nuclear weapons of its own. It is a small country lying between East and West, in the heart of Europe. Its inhabitants feel threatened and after forty years are once again afraid of war. You know as well as I that every single family in your country and in ours suffered in the war, so we share a mutual interest in avoiding a new war."

It was clear to me, however, that the discussion of medium-range missiles could get no further at this time and place; the gap dividing us was still insurmountable in April 1985. I tried instead to focus on the economic bonds between our two countries. I continued:

"I regard economic interdependence as an extremely important way of preventing war. That was one reason why Deutsche Bank made a point of not breaking off talks with Soviet negotiators when our two countries were officially not on speaking terms because of certain well-known events. Incidentally, West Germany is a reliable partner not just politically but also economically. The whole world knows how dependable we are about sticking to agreements."

Gorbachev picked up on my cue. "Our economic ties with West Germany can certainly be broadened. In my opinion we can make up for our trade setbacks of last winter and spring. We are facing a number of new problems, especially in regard to stepping up scientific and technological progress. The latter requires new ideas from all of us. However, when the West Germans send us their exports, they should not try to send us outmoded goods. That is the goal of the COCOM* list and the protectionist policy."

I replied that German technology was in demand throughout

* The Coordinating Committee of the Paris Consultative Group (COCOM) controls the exports of strategic materials or equipment to communist countries.

the world. It wasn't cheap, I said, but its quality was of the first class. West Germany couldn't possibly maintain its world market position if it delivered outmoded goods.

Gorbachev said: "I just wanted to say it for the record."

In the course of our dialogue, we both came to the following conclusion: The Soviet Union, with its enormous natural resources, and West Germany, with its high technology, would complement each other ideally in the area of economic exchange. When our conversation turned to the economic strength of Japan and West Germany, it again became obvious that our minds were still dominated by questions of military strategy.

Gorbachev: "Japan and West Germany have spent less on rearming, and that's why their economies are stronger. Now West Germany wants the Western European Union* to have all weapons systems at its disposal. That is dangerous. The Soviet Union is keeping a close watch on this development."

I stated emphatically: "No one on our side wants to jeopardize peace!"

Gorbachev countered: "Do the Germans really need new lessons?"

I forcefully repeated: "We have no nuclear weapons of our own. Our arms exports are minor. But we are a NATO country just as East Germany is a member of the Warsaw Pact. This gives us security and it should not cause distrust."

Gorbachev's tone became distinctly more conciliatory: "I spent years living with Moslems in the Caucasus. The Moslems have a saying: 'It does not hurt to repeat a prayer.'"

Gorbachev then focused on the historical closeness of our two cultures. He voiced his regret that he had visited West Germany only once, in 1975, at the invitation of the German Communist Party, to attend the celebration marking the thirtieth anniversary of the end of World War II. He told me about a significant experi-

* The Western European Union, a defense alliance between France, West Germany, the Benelux countries, and Great Britain, was formed chiefly to control West German rearmament.

ence he had had while driving. He and his retinue had to stop at a small gas station. Getting out, they chatted while stretching their legs. Suddenly the somewhat elderly gas station owner asked them if they were Russians. When they said yes, the man grew very earnest and explicitly attacked the Soviet Union because it had divided his country, Germany. He also said that the Soviets had caused his family a lot of suffering. Gorbachev then asked the man if they could go indoors and respond to his accusations. And that was what they did. Gorbachev made it clear to the man that the Western Allies had consolidated their three zones into a single partial state to oppose the Soviet Union. Thus, no one could blame the Soviet Union for causing the division of Germany.

This story reminds me of a comment supposedly made by Stalin at the Yalta Conference in February 1945. The gist of it (according to a document preserved at the historic conference room in Yalta) was that the large German nation cannot remain divided forever. We must add that Stalin wanted to keep an undivided Germany under Communist rule. In any case, Mikhail Gorbachev's encounter at the German gas station must have made a lasting impact on him. He described it again later on during his official visit to West Germany in June 1989.

As I have said, Gorbachev and I spoke quite frankly when we met. His hostility toward the United States kept seeping through even though he never once mentioned President Reagan by name. My previous experiences in all the regions and with the media of the enormous Soviet Union had been very different. No one had ever hesitated to inveigh against specific public figures when talking about the United States. By the time I had my conversation with Gorbachev, Moscow had unilaterally halted its underground nuclear tests as an advance concession for détente talks, and it asked the United States to do the same. In discussing this with me, Gorbachev went through the entire litany of the Soviet Union's misgivings and its persistently cultivated distrust of the Americans.

Trying to parry his rebukes, I pointed out that the United States and NATO were acting on the basis of many years of coping with the arms policies of the Soviet Union and the Warsaw Pact nations. Their conduct had repeatedly given the West ample reason to handle Moscow's pronouncements with care. That, I said, was why mountains of mutual distrust had been growing between the two sides, and those mountains could be worn down only by means of laborious efforts and infinite patience. My experiences in the Soviet Union had taught me, I said, that personal encounters would be the primary conditions for developing a basis of mutual trust.

I then stated: "Mr. Gorbachev, even in your stringently and centrally ruled" (the word *dictatorial* was on the tip of my tongue, but I managed to stifle it) "country, you cannot order your citizens to be trustful, and it is even less possible in a democratic structure like that of America." Pointing to Vladimir Alkhimov who was sitting next to Gorbachev, I described the distrust, indeed virtual hostility, with which I had been received during my first encounters in Moscow. Since then, I went on, our frequent talks and our steady efforts toward a mutually advantageous association had led to reciprocal understanding and trust, which I now regarded as a fundamental achievement that would benefit both sides. Gorbachev looked pensive.

All in all it struck me that this new general secretary was a good listener. Though he asked tough questions, he was nevertheless intent on learning from outsiders and not just his own advisers— as shown by the following example. Gorbachev complained that West Germany was surrendering its own interests to those of the United States. Vast amounts of our financial resources—for instance, the savings deposits of our citizens—were being transferred to America, he said, to cover its huge federal budget deficits. As a result the investments necessary for the West German economy could no longer be financed.

I replied that this simply did not agree with the facts. From my own observations I knew that many West Germans were paying considerable sums for United States treasury notes, but we must remember that every West German citizen has complete freedom over his savings and can invest them in foreign currency and in any country of his choice. If many German investors now preferred sending their money to America, then their action was completely voluntary, and there were two reasons for their decision: The U.S. dollar was in demand as an alternative currency, and the future development of the American economy looked extremely promising.

Gorbachev was clearly impressed by my explanation, but he was also disgruntled because he had obviously been misled. At any rate, this was the only time during our long conversation that he frowned, pulled his glasses from their case, and glanced down at a list on which a number of items were underlined in red. Previously he had simply kept transferring his glasses case from hand to hand, fervently emphasizing his statements. I realized that the adviser responsible for misinforming him could expect a scolding—and rightly so.

I had assumed that our conversation would touch mainly on economic issues and perhaps also on some specific projects that I had been successfully negotiating for years, but this was not the case. Mikhail Gorbachev was clearly intent on staying with the basic issues. At one point I mentioned that a lot of energy and raw materials were being squandered in his country. This was also true, I added, of some machinery and equipment that had been purchased with costly Western currency.

My comments clearly struck a raw nerve in Gorbachev, underscoring his own observations. I expected him to rebuff me for my harsh criticism, but he did the exact opposite: He heartily agreed with me. In later talks he often referred to this issue when he discussed economic planning and the achievement of scheduled goals. The general secretary was obviously aware of the weaknesses in the Five-Year Plan and in the planning commissions. Resources, he said, had to be deployed more efficiently. Also, five-year periods were too short for long-term restructuring; a plan should run for at least ten years. Indeed, very soon after taking over his enormous responsibilities, Gorbachev assailed mismanagement, and he was not afraid of personal consequences when he introduced changes in the traditional planning system.

By and large our detailed conversation left me with a positive impression of a man who had resolved to bring about radical transformations after years of observing his country's system. He was determined to wipe out a kind of acquiescent immobilism that had been cultivated to ward off any unwelcome modifications—that is, any threat to the existing power structure.

My impression was subsequently confirmed by a preeminent source; namely, some senior advisers in Gorbachev's immediate entourage. When I informed these men of my rather critical observations of the Brezhnev era, they agreed with me completely. But they added that as of 1970 they themselves had kept meticulous notes on misjudgments and mismanagement and then submitted their findings to Yuri Andropov when he took office in 1982.

Thus, my first meeting with Gorbachev made a deep impact on me: I was impressed by him personally and by the substance of our talk. In April 1985, the new master of the Kremlin was still generally unknown, even in the Soviet Union. When I returned home from our meeting, journalists asked me: "What kind of man is he?" I could only reply: "If anyone can change that country, he can!"

My Soviet counterparts, with whom I was negotiating even more intensely, also wanted to hear my impression of their new top man since they had not yet met him. I said that both sides— the Soviet Union and other countries—could expect a great deal from this new general secretary. His personal charisma, the candor in his vivid brown eyes, his straightforward conversation and analysis—all these had made our encounter exciting for me. Prime Minister Margaret Thatcher had a similar experience when, in December 1984, several weeks before Gorbachev took office, the two of them met for extensive talks in London.

When Gorbachev became general secretary, his first official foreign visit was in the fall of 1985. His destination, Paris, had a symbolic meaning, of course. At his closing press conference hundreds of journalists from all over the world were sitting at his feet, and the international press described him as being completely different from all his predecessors: open-minded and sophisticated.

Much as I agreed, initially I was caught off guard by these adjectives that were being applied to him so early. I wanted to track down the source of his worldliness. Aside from visits to Eastern European satellite states, Gorbachev had done little foreign traveling. Prior to his official visit in Paris, he had been to England, as I have mentioned, to Canada in 1983, and to West Germany in 1975 when the German Communist Party had invited him to their celebration of the thirtieth anniversary of the end of World War II. I was able to compile further data about him: In his youth Gorbachev had been exposed to interesting influences while studying for two degrees. First, he went through the full five years of law school in Moscow. Then, from his native region in the Caucasian foothills, he completed an equally long correspondence course in agriculture (Soviet correspondence courses are strictly supervised.) During his student days in Moscow, Gorbachev had supposedly maintained close ties with Zdeněk Mlynář from Czechoslovakia. Later on, during the Prague Spring of 1968, Mlynář became a sort of chief ideologue for Alexander Dubcek who wanted to introduce a socialism with a human face into his country. Czechs and Slovaks have always considered themselves Central Europeans, both historically and spiritually. It takes little imagination to realize how deeply the twenty-year-old Gorbachev was influenced by the ideas and concepts of Mlynář, his enterprising fellow student. Back then, Gorbachev may have already developed his distinct knack for critical probing and analyzing, for drawing conclusions and translating them into practical policies. Today this gift is coupled with a natural talent for dealing openly with people and expressing his thoughts in a persuasive style.

In the summer of 1985 a typical story about Gorbachev made the rounds in Moscow. The new general secretary was about to take an utterly inconceivable step: He wanted to talk to the man in the street in a relaxed and informal way. He turned up unannounced in Moscow suburbs to address workers in factories and cafeterias. During a visit in Leningrad he strolled unescorted along the crowded boulevards conversing with passersby. Imagine the excitement of the TV teams that went dashing there!

That evening when Gorbachev watched the main news telecast, there was no mention of his stroll. It turned out that any public appearance by a top Soviet leader had always been thoroughly checked out if not manipulated prior to being aired. Any appearances shown of the Party secretary had to be according to the Party line, but the new man's conduct was so unusual that the Kremlin had to apply vigorous pressure to get the media accustomed to these new practices.

No one had ever had to think about the correct media presentation of the top hierarchy. Neither Brezhnev nor Khrushchev, and certainly not Stalin, had ever behaved even remotely like Gorbachev. Stalin, the "Old Master," had seldom spoken on the radio, nor had he appeared on television (which was still in its infancy when he died in 1953). His posturing was unsuitable for those media, as was his bizarre diction with its strong Georgian accent. Besides, it was intrinsic to the system, even in czarist times, that the ruler have an unapproachable aura and be glimpsed only from a distance. Brezhnev was incapable of speaking freely in public and followed the tradition of the potentates of Greater Russia.

As a result, the open, uncomplicated manner of Mikhail Gorbachev was regarded as new and sensational. The media representatives, the officials, and certainly the public were completely bewildered. Centuries of czarism and then seventy years of Soviet rule had been brutally and violently forced on the people, creating an almost slavish obeisance. On the other hand, this absolute allegiance and servility had produced a feeling of safety and security in personal dependence. But now Gorbachev was calling on the Soviets to throw off their fears and traditional submissiveness and to take charge of their own lives. This challenge was novel and perplexing; it would take a long time to comprehend it.

Meanwhile, Gorbachev has perfected an impressive image, demonstrating that he is his own best public relations officer. His words, deeds, and gestures reveal that he is not playing any well-rehearsed role and that courage, intelligence, and persuasiveness are intrinsic to his personality. He is capable of both tact and impatience. The general apathy in his country must cause him almost physical suffering. Gorbachev is, without a doubt, a highly gifted politician, and the people around him can only learn from him.

His image is enhanced by his wife Raisa, whose assistance is quite unusual for a Soviet leader's spouse. Anyone who converses with her soon realizes that this former philosophy teacher is no mere window dressing; fully on a par with her husband, she is quite capable of representing her country abroad. Equally uncomplicated in direct dealings with people, she remains relaxed and self-assured even in hectic surroundings, such as a chaotic onslaught of journalists and photographers.

Gorbachev is second to none in speaking to and about his people. For him, glasnost means exposing problems and setting goals. His openness naturally inspired the man in the street to look forward to improvements in the supply situation of food and consumer goods, but the longer such elementary hopes stay unfulfilled, the greater the danger of general unrest in the population. And then, of course, comparisons are made with earlier times. Those periods were not exactly rosy, but the supply system was slightly better. As a result, there is widespread and justifiable anxiety in the West that Gorbachev's reform efforts might be doomed. And certain Soviet functionaries who found their lives comfortable under previous regimes may even be desirous of Gorbachev's failure.

The general secretary is faced with stubborn opponents of reformism, an economy in shambles, a corrupt and paralyzing bureaucracy, an alarming mismanagement of social resources, and ethnic conflicts that used to be violently suppressed. These factors comprise tensions in which the "new thinking" must prove itself. Its goals, according to Gorbachev, are "a new morality, a new psychology," that require the individual to share responsibility for the world of tomorrow, "if it ever comes about." Time is running out, and nobody knows that better than Gorbachev himself.

11 · A UNIQUE PEACE CONGRESS

One of Mikhail Gorbachev's most spectacular efforts to advance the cause of détente in East-West relations was his "Peace Congress," which originally elicited a few smirks. It took place in Moscow during February 1987. Among the hundreds of participants representing all races and nations, we members of the business and economic community were perhaps the only ones with clear-cut future goals.

The entire event had been carefully prepared over a long period of time. Back in the fall of 1986 while attending an international conference on fundamental economic policies, I had been approached about the Peace Congress and invited to take part. I hesitated because I was given no information about its program and agenda despite my numerous requests. By accepting I might have run the risk of co-signing a declaration that I had not helped to formulate. This had occurred often enough in the past: Well-meaning and perhaps naive participants in Soviet-sponsored peace celebrations had had the dubious distinction of finding their names endorsing questionable or vaguely worded texts.

The organizers obviously set great store by my presence. But since I was distrustful, I stipulated that I would sign no public statement and that any declarations I made would be left intact and published verbatim. I asked for and received an unequivocal promise to that effect, and the promise was kept. I was not put on the spot even once during the conference. This, too, was new. As I have mentioned, my earlier experiences were quite different.

The congress also brought together people of different persuasions with the most disparate views. These groups came from around the world, and few if any were officials of a government. The participants who stood out the most visually were representatives of religious groups, usually orthodox in character.

The discussion groups met at the Trade Center, which had been designed by the American millionaire Armand Hammer in the style of American exhibition sites. Most of the visitors were staying at the hotel connected to the center. In the corridors you could see countless churchmen in their flowing robes, each bishop holding a crozier and wearing a lofty miter atop a bearded face. Their dignified gait seemed out of place in that hustle and bustle. Those of us in plain clothes formed a much smaller contingent, and we felt almost like intruders—like gray church mice in that ceremonious environment. There were sociologists and physicians, psychologists and philosophers, peace researchers and ex-generals, writers and actors, such as Gregory Peck and Marcello Mastroianni. I met the Italian actor one evening in a colorful group of international artists who had been invited by the Soviet Artists' Association to take part in a very blunt, almost boisterous exchange of ideas with painters from Azerbaijan and Armenia.

This was quite in keeping with Gorbachev's plan. The new head of the Kremlin wanted to get beyond the official talks and trading of views by professional politicians. In front of an international forum, he was virtually laying out the basic guidelines of a new politics that would be rigorously different from earlier Soviet goals and methods. The concluding event was held at the Kremlin's beautiful Catherine Hall. Here in the presence of Andrei Sakharov, winner of the Nobel Peace Prize, Gorbachev spoke about a spiritual revolution which would make people realize that all human beings now share a common fate.

People in Moscow frequently asked me for my impressions,

hoping I would tell them what effect this unique conference would have. Such perceptions are hard to capture in a few words. I was familiar enough with Gorbachev's mentality not to be surprised by what he said. I have already described his outlook. This outstanding statesman is first and foremost a Soviet patriot; I believe he sees the Soviet Union and the world far beyond the present day, even into the next century, with all the risks and opportunities that will open up for his gigantic country on a global scale. In addition to his conference being a huge public relations success, his statements made an impact. The participants felt that his "new thinking" was meant to bring about a different kind of Soviet Union, one that would at least turn its back on seventy years of Soviet ideology with its claim to world domination. At this point, however, the rest of the world will have to wait and see what develops. After decades of negative experiences with the Soviets, the members of the various study groups from East and West were curious to hear the unusual proclamations at the Moscow Peace Congress, but they took them with a grain of salt.

The economic forum was certainly the most down-to-earth part of the congress. Its participants represented nearly all the COMECON nations as well as the European Economic Community, the United States, and Japan. The Soviet Union mobilized its top economists as well as its leading functionaries of business and trade. The Americans expressed more frustration than anything else. Some of these businessmen announced that they were capable and desirous of practicing greater cooperation, but the administration in Washington hampered their involvement. I was surprised because large numbers of prominent Americans had always participated in various meetings with the Soviets; they had gotten together within the framework of joint economic commissions both in Washington and Moscow. I had learned about this from Ronald Reagan's confidant, Commerce Secretary Malcolm Baldridge.

During two visits in Washington I had met with Baldridge to

exchange views on Moscow's reform efforts. While not agreeing on everything, we shared some basic beliefs. I really liked this athletic gentleman—as horseman to horseman, so to speak. At his office he proudly showed me the rodeo saddle on display next to his desk. He had won it in a rodeo at the age of sixty. But his passion proved fatal for him; he was subsequently killed in a rodeo accident.

The Japanese were distinctly aggressive in Moscow. They single-mindedly presented their expectations of sharing new and major projects with the Soviet Union. I will return to this later.

As for our wishes, I brought up three items that I felt were especially important; most of my Soviet counterparts were already acquainted with them from earlier discussions. The first point called for joint ventures, each between a Western and a Soviet enterprise. Similar projects had already been implemented in China during the early eighties; German firms had gained a wealth of experience by working with Chinese enterprises in Canton (Kwangchow), a province bordering Hong Kong. We regarded these joint ventures as highly instructive.

In earlier years I had frequently approached the Soviets about such projects; citing examples from Hungary and Bulgaria, I had offered to help determine whether those possibilities would be of value in the Soviet economy. During the pre-Gorbachev period my recommendations were ignored, but as of 1986 they were suddenly welcomed as ideas to be instituted without delay. Gorbachev, as we know, is also striving to revamp Soviet foreign trade. He would like to export smaller amounts of natural resources such as oil and gas and instead supply Western countries with products that have a higher profit margin, especially machinery. In response to our suggestions, the top leadership decided that this structural change could best be implemented and maintained by joint ventures between the Soviets and Western partners. All at once a proposal that had previously been rejected was now considered a brainstorm. The English term "joint venture" became a buzzword.

At the Moscow forum I urged the Soviets to be patient. A joint venture, I explained, is the most demanding form of coopera-tion—a crowning achievement—and it can materialize only on a step-by-step basis. It was no use, I said, resorting to the methods employed in fulfilling a plan, that is, demonstrating as many projects as possible. Instead, the numerous and varied prerequi-sites of each project had to be dealt with. Since a huge number of West German firms were already enjoying good relations with Soviet firms and their top management, I suggested that the Sovi-ets begin with those West German companies. The first step would be to examine, case by case, whether a broader cooperation was possible. I compared the process to a courtship: The two parties should start by getting engaged, as it were, in order to find out what they had in common. After mutually checking to see whether the relationship was solid enough for a joint venture, they could then formally settle on a cooperative undertaking that was desired by both parties.

Since that conference, the fundamental interest in joint ven-tures has greatly increased. The Western firms evidently are hop-ing to build a solid foundation for what promises to be a gigantic market in the Soviet Union. On the other hand, these firms realize that they cannot embark on such ventures without metic-ulous investigation and consultation; a great deal of managerial and financial know-how is required. Nor can these firms rule out the possibility that their exports might be jeopardized by the marketing of their joint-venture products.

The second item on my conference agenda was the problem of consultation. Earlier large-scale Soviet investments for imports of Western machines or facilities had often failed to achieve their goals. Valuable products that were paid for with billions in hard currency had not been put to use, ending up in various garbage dumps somewhere in this vast country. I therefore reprised my suggestion that in such cases the Soviets should hire competent industrial consulting firms in the West. I offered my audience a plausible argument: Of course, professional consulting costs

money, but if you weigh this expense against the losses caused
by bad or inefficient investments and factor in the time wasted
on making changes or adjustments, you will see that the additional outlay for a professional consulting firm is more than
justified. But ultimately, no matter how often I articulated this
fundamental idea, no matter how much acceptance it found in
the ministries and other agencies, the Soviets always came up
with counterarguments and ignored my recommendation. The
chief reason for their reluctance may have been that the category
of "consulting fee" did not exist in their planning budgets. Perhaps they also distrusted this "capitalist" method, suspecting
some gimmick that would burden the socialist partner with additional overhead.

My third and final point concerned the Soviet banking system,
which I had been familiar with for quite a while. Citing the
restructuring plans, which were constantly brought up at the
forum, I proposed that the Soviets modify and diversify the traditional banking structure so that it could handle the new tasks.
These changes were worked on until 1987, and one year later a
new system was introduced. The main feature of the reform is
that the previously all-powerful Gosbank has been transformed
into what is purely a central bank with the task of controlling
currency. Now there are special banks for specific services, including agriculture, personal savings, and home construction.
Although still fledgling institutions, they do their best to advise
the average Soviet citizen and are gradually developing professional competency. The old Foreign Trade Bank has become the
Bank for Foreign Economic Affairs, and its status has been up-
graded. It now has the decisive role in cooperation with Western
firms, such as joint ventures, and in negotiating and utilizing
credits from Western countries.

12 · TRAVELS TO THE SECRET REGIONS OF THE SOVIET WORLD

In the fall of 1988, the Soviets invited me to take an exploratory trip to the Kola Peninsula. And for a "Westerner" like me, it was an exploration in the truest sense of the word.

Moscow was gradually starting to reveal its secret areas to Western eyes. And Kola, the legendary gigantic peninsula in the far north between the White Sea and the Barents Sea, is such a region. Until recently this once fiercely contested neighbor of Finland had been a restricted military zone and therefore excluded from discussions of German-Soviet development ventures.

The naval port of Murmansk is located here; during the past few decades it has undergone a tremendous expansion—not only for naval purposes, incidentally, but for civilian purposes as well. Although it lies north of the Arctic Circle, because of the Gulf Stream, Murmansk is the only port on the northern Soviet coast to remain ice-free all year long. Together with Kola, Murmansk is a hub in the vast Soviet network of top-secret military installations. One received only the vaguest hints that, because of its convenient geographical location in regard to the United States, this area had a strong concentration of launching pads for intercontinental missiles as well as bases for submarines and long-distance bombers. In fact, Murmansk was vital to the Soviets during World War II. Since its harbor never freezes over, the huge cargoes of lend-lease military equipment that President Roosevelt had agreed to provide were unloaded here.

In the fall of 1988, when I entered the city that had long been off limits to foreigners, I suddenly recalled an episode that had occurred in the summer of 1942. At that time, as the Wehrmacht launched its second major summer offensive toward the Don and the Volga, we were stationed between Kursk and Voronesh on the Don. Here we first discovered that Soviet troops were carrying American food cans, and later on we noted that their weapons were marked "Made in the USA." We learned this matériel was being shipped to the southern Russian front via the North Atlantic and Murmansk. It was obvious, even to a low-ranking, twenty-year-old officer like myself, that the war had taken a decisive turn when the United States had joined on the side of the Soviet Union.

The West knew the Kola Peninsula was not just rumored to be a Soviet military zone, but it also contained mammoth deposits of natural resources. It was not until after General Secretary Gorbachev's visit here in the fall of 1987, however, that these raw materials were to be tapped for future civilian planning. Beyond its military importance, Kola had already undergone some development in industry, mining, and shipping, while the Murmansk area had become a major fishing center. But the general secretary felt that the peninsula was a long way from taking full advantage of its industrial potential.

On October 1, 1987, Mikhail Gorbachev, as I have already mentioned, addressed the workers and senior functionaries of Murmansk. His keynote speech, later translated into the various Soviet and also a few Western languages, was circulated as a brochure throughout the U.S.S.R. When I visited Murmansk, I was repeatedly questioned about his speech: What was so important about it? I was told that it had virtually ignited the vast industrial reforms and effective development of this entire region, which had previously been restricted by its military isolation.

Gorbachev's speech contained two major points. First of all, the new general secretary kept impressing upon his listeners that they should not always wait for orders from Moscow if a different method turns out to be more efficient than the one decreed; instead, the local people should use their own judgment in deciding what was best. As I have already said, the management personnel have been instructed to follow those new guidelines.

Flexibility has never been known or tolerated here, and it will be quite a while before it takes root. This shows how wide the gap still is between Gorbachev's demand and the Soviet reality. Nevertheless, I must admit that one can observe more and more exceptions from the lethargy, even resignation that have characterized Soviet officials for such a long time. I have attended management seminars at which some of the young Soviets appeared so brilliant that we West German participants jokingly debated which of them we might have recruited as executive trainees.

Gorbachev's second point concerned government subsidies, a troublesome theme for us too. The general secretary bewailed the fact that his country was spending 70 billion rubles ($83.5 billion at the then-current exchange rate) a year to subsidize rents and basic food items. This outlay, he said, was no longer tolerable and would have to be reduced.

One can only agree with his conclusion. The military complex and the government subsidies are without a doubt the primary items in the overall Soviet budget. When I was made aware of this point in Gorbachev's speech, I couldn't help thinking that these concerns were shared by politicians in the East and West alike, and I felt it might be a good time to mention the cuts in military spending that are desired by both NATO and the Warsaw Pact nations. Gorbachev repeatedly announced that the U.S.S.R. would reveal aspects of its military budget as soon as both sides agreed on which details should be pinpointed for an honest comparison.

Gorbachev's visit in October 1987 highlighted Kola and Murmansk, impelling the local officials to increase their efforts; they intend to exploit the wealth of local resources and even bring a tourist trade to this stark yet charming area. From the very outset they are obviously relying on Western help. In any case, it was probably because of these new plans that in the spring of 1988, just a few months after Gorbachev's speech, I received an invitation from Premier Nikolai Y. Ryzhkov. He asked me not only to take an educational trip to Kola but also to determine possible ways in which Soviet authorities could work with West German firms. This invitation, which I acted on in the autumn of 1988, indicated to me that the military function of the Kola area no longer had top priority.

Honored as I was by the Soviet premier's proposal, it was a highly complicated matter. We completed a phase in which German firms had been forced to endure all kinds of setbacks in their dealings with the Soviets. In the spring of 1988, the Soviet Union's largest business contract with foreign partners had been signed without German participation. This was the so-called Tengis Project, an enormous plan to extract the natural resources near the Caspian Sea, with an estimated volume of about $6 billion. The firm in charge is Occidental Petroleum, known because of Dr. Armand Hammer, the grand old man of East-West business dealings.

Hammer, now over ninety years old, can look back on a marvelous track record. As a student he shook Lenin's hand, and for decades this made the American an almost legendary figure in Moscow. He was a genius at exploiting this reputation commercially. Starting in the early 1920s he has known every Soviet Party chief personally, and he has accordingly offered every American president his services as mediator. I have always had a soft spot in my heart for this unusual and rather controversial figure.

As the Tengis Project showed, Hammer had once again pulled off a coup by playing on Moscow's admiration for his prestigious past accomplishments. The co-signatories included Italians and Japanese but no Germans. Several German firms did try to obtain subcontracts by doing a vast amount of preliminary work, but from 1985 to 1987 the Soviets, at Gorbachev's behest, implemented a virtually all-embracing cancellation of orders. For one thing, before launching his reform policies Gorbachev evidently wanted to take inventory; for another thing, the dollar was falling and so were oil prices—which spelled billions of dollars in losses for Soviet exports of primary energy, that is, oil and natural gas. It was only in 1988 that Moscow lifted its restrictions on contracts with the West. Now, after years of wasted efforts, the German firms understandably wanted to use the opportunity.

Long in advance I had made an appointment with Premier Ryzhkov for an overall stock-taking, hoping to discuss the full range of German interests. Scheduling problems kept getting in the way, but eventually we managed to agree on a Saturday morning in the spring of 1988 when we could talk undisturbed and without a time limit.

Ryzhkov's personality is completely different from his predecessor's. While Nikolai Tikhonov was stern, very earnest, and ideologically hampered, Nikolai Ryzhkov seems Anglo-Saxon in type: open and relaxed, businesslike, and predictable.

When I broached the subject of German firms, the premier assured me in a manner both amiable and resolute that while the Soviets acknowledged the quality and reliability of West German enterprises, other Western and also Japanese firms were more flexible; this simply meant their terms were more favorable.

However, several weeks later, thanks to Armand Hammer's intervention, Ryzhkov made me an offer: a joint venture involving an even bigger project in central Siberia. In order to keep a scheduled appointment at the Kremlin, I flew to Moscow with Armand Hammer in his private jet, a generously but not luxuriously appointed Boeing 727.

The immense project included the transporting of vast quantities of crude petroleum from northern Siberia to Nizhnevartovsk, a city some thirteen hundred miles northeast of Moscow with a population of 100,000. The oil was to be converted into derivatives as well as all sorts of chemical base products, which would then either be sent abroad or else undergo further processing by various Soviet industries. To import the items needed to do the processing, specific licenses were needed from the West German chemical industry.

This made a lot of sense for the Soviets. Gorbachev wanted a complete overhaul of the Soviet export system. Instead of being sold to other countries, raw materials would be processed inside the Soviet Union, assuring them of the biggest possible profit margin. However, most of the required licenses were for products that had been developed at a tremendous cost for research by German companies that wanted to maintain their competitive edge on an international level. As a result, despite long and vigorous talks, this American-German-Soviet cooperation, which would have opened up a huge central Siberian region, fizzled out. It was the Japanese who finally clinched the deal.

Naturally there were times during years of negotiations when the Germans were checkmated. We always carefully analyzed the reasons for each failure in order to learn from it and also to offer useful advice to the participating German manufacturers. Occasionally, however, we were unable to fathom the real causes. Even when we felt that the German offer was fully consistent with Soviet wishes in both price and quality, we had to take the prevailing political situation into account. This meant that when political tensions arose, commerce was deliberately shunted aside, and vice versa.

Since political reasons were very seldom cited explicitly, we often could only guess at the truth. For example, major Italian firms were involved in the huge Tengis Project because Bettino Craxi, the Italian prime minister, had a direct tie with Gorbachev, and the Soviets wanted to make a political gesture. The large-scale expansion of the Moscow trade center was a different but equally political case. In 1988 a well-known German construction firm had submitted a conclusive bid that was high in both price and quality. Then we heard that this prestigious contract was to be awarded to a Yugoslav firm—partly, no doubt, for political reasons. That very spring Mikhail Gorbachev had spent several days on a state visit in Belgrade, hoping to put an end to Moscow's conflicts with the Socialist sister nation that had been going its own way since the Tito regime. Gorbachev's mission was generally successful. Throughout the years we had often talked about the economic and financial situations of individual Eastern bloc countries and the possibilities of providing them with joint East-West assistance. I had been repeatedly advised that Moscow no longer felt called upon to solve Yugoslavia's problems; it was now up to the West. There was no mistaking Moscow's open repudiation of Belgrade.

Anyhow, we now had to safeguard German business interests in Kola. When I visited the peninsula in September 1988, I was delighted to note how receptive all the local authorities were, from the top administrators in Murmansk to the local scientists, the technicians, and the commercial managers in factories.

No matter with whom I spoke, they all realized that an intensive development of the natural wealth in this area could not succeed without technological and financial help from the West. A previous collaboration with their neighbor Finland had evidently not met with the desired success. I noticed that the abandonment of centralized thinking at Gorbachev's suggestion—indeed, orders—was being pursued here with a zeal to be found only in genuine pioneers. Away from the Moscow ministries and on to self-reliance in action and responsibility!

The participants in the Kola venture could already cite a pertinent decree issued by Moscow's Council of Ministers. But meanwhile there are still a few snags in the actual implementation. There is often no way of telling if and how many ministries are in charge of a given project. The awareness of the central power is lodged so deeply in Soviet minds that it will be quite a while before it disappears altogether.

But from which angles can we approach a collaboration in Kola? First of all, we have to ask a preliminary question: How can the wealth of Kola be harnessed for the European Common Market, an area lying relatively close to the Soviet Union? The peninsula is rich in natural resources, some of which are rare and currently must be imported to Europe from South Africa and Australia. I had already discussed in Moscow the effects of exporting Kola's raw materials to the West, pointing out that we would be dealing with long-range perspectives requiring a great deal of patience.

There can be no doubt that the Soviets are quite serious about developing Kola. In Murmansk and Moscow I was presented with an investment plan amounting to 18 billion rubles ($21.5 billion at the then-current exchange rate). Projected to run until the end the century, this plan also covers infrastructure improvements and individual investments.

If this concentration of natural resources is to be exploited in a joint venture with the West, then we already have a geographic head start in regard to transportation. Two routes are possible: The northern one begins in the ice-free port of Murmansk and runs around the North Cape to the North Sea and the Common Market countries. The southern inland waterway, passing through the lakes and canals of the Soviet republic of Karelia, goes to the Baltic Sea and the ports of Leningrad and Kaliningrad in Russia and Lübeck in Germany. This latter course seems to be arousing more interest.

When talking to local officials in Petrozavodsk, the Karelian capital, I could sense that this barely industrialized area on the Finnish border hopes to profit from the development of Kola. Furthermore, Karelia is planning to make its natural beauties desirable to Western tourists and their foreign currency.

Petrozavodsk, scenically located on the vast reaches of Lake Onega, would be a delightful starting point for Western European hunters and fishermen who could revel in its unspoiled landscape. This town was created in 1703 by Peter the Great who set up a foundry here to cast the cannon for his Baltic fleet, which battled his archenemy, Charles XII of Sweden. On a small island in the lake you will find Kizhi, a museum village with marvelous wooden churches from the eighteenth century—a treasure trove for lovers of Russian Orthodox art. Catherine the Great was so fond of Petrozavodsk that she built herself a small summer château here.

The backbone for industrializing the region is to be a gigantic hydroelectric plant planned for construction near the Finnish border. Its projected capacity of four thousand megawatts would make it the largest non-nuclear facility in Europe, offering cheap power to Kola in the north, Karelia in the south, and Finland in the west. But environmental activists, especially in Finland, are already up in arms about the large-scale destruction of the virgin forest.

Ecological awareness is mounting in the Soviet Union. Since 1988, Mikhail Gorbachev has repeatedly emphasized the need to protect natural resources. His conduct is unprecedented. During my earlier Soviet travels I could observe how even an elementary respect for nature was being ignored throughout this vast country. In some regions I saw terrifying devastation that made the surface of the moon seem hospitable by comparison. The lunar landscape has always looked like that; but the earth is being destroyed by man. In Kola I also found the land laid to waste by mining and by ruthless exploitation of resources. The government plans to spend an enormous portion of its budget of 18 billion rubles on reforesting this area. Unfortunately, the climate will make such efforts inadequate and very slow.

I wanted to make my own personal contribution to the development of the massive Kola project. In March 1989, at the first German-Soviet Forum in Bad Godesberg, I spoke to Professor Leonid Abalkin, Gorbachev's economic adviser. I suggested establishing an "industrial Baltic Region K" where special tax and investment incentives would be offered to create an industrial and technological center for joint German-Soviet ventures. The letter K stands for the city of Kaliningrad, which was called Königsberg until 1945.

This city lies on the Soviet route that I have already discussed—the "southern" water route from the Kola Peninsula to Lübeck. This would give Kaliningrad a pivotal function. In making my proposal I deliberately referred to Gorbachev's image of "the common European house." If this is not to remain a mere figure of speech, as Helmut Schmidt recently put it, the house must be filled with life and made more comprehensible to the nations in the East and West alike. My exact words were that such a visionary concept can become a reality only "if past problems are solved, present borders eliminated, and future goals realized." One such future goal would be Baltic Region K.

Getting down to specifics, I pointed out that a favorable transportation infrastructure already existed in Odessa, the Black Sea city where the first step toward a similar project had already been taken. Kaliningrad has short and fast sea and land connections to Poland and East Germany as well as Scandinavia and Western Europe. Raw materials from Kola would reach the processing plants here immediately. The former territory of East Prussia is culturally closer to the Germans than remote Siberia, and that would probably make the location more acceptable to German workers. I assured my Soviet interlocutors that the project should not be misconstrued as a German attempt at using cold economic ploys to reoccupy a historically problematic region.* Rather, the nearness of different joint ventures within a small geographic space would create something that we know is sought by young pioneer enterprises: a platform for an exchange of ideas and experiences.

I also suggested that an institute of technology, ecology, and science, with a special department for joint ventures, should be established nearby; its purpose would be to speed up the conversion of theory into technological practice. Finally, I spoke about various other aspects: the social infrastructure with its various

---

* In July 1990 we were told by Ivan S. Zilayev, the new premier of the Russian Federation, that this anxiety had been increased by the imminent reunification of Germany. I managed to put his mind at ease. Such motives would discredit the K plan from the very start.

appeals for Germans and Russians willing to work in the area; a training center that could offer consulting services throughout the Soviet Union; and small- and medium-sized ancillary businesses. I also proposed setting up a free trade zone which would provide powerful impulses for an industrialization policy; this would be a semi-autonomous region under Soviet sovereignty.

We should not underestimate, I said, either the economic importance of such a project or its political effect. For the West European, especially the West German, this would be a frank commitment to a common European future symbolized by the free trade zone of Kaliningrad. On the German side, cooperation would be a resounding response to the questions raised about "Königsberg." It would confirm that this is a Soviet city—an attitude that I believe reflects the West German consensus.

Incidentally, I would like to add that the new Soviet citizens of Kaliningrad are increasingly discovering the history of their region for themselves. Immanuel Kant, the great son of this city (and the German philosopher second only to Georg Wilhelm Friedrich Hegel in recognition among the Russians), is increasingly mentioned with respect.

During the mid-seventies there was a long debate about making the Kaliningrad area the site of German-Soviet cooperation. After the 1973–74 oil crisis, West Germany wanted to participate in the expansion of Europe's biggest nuclear energy center in order to safeguard its supply of electric power. In October 1974, during Helmut Schmidt's official visit to Moscow in which I took part, this project was specifically discussed, but the plan was thwarted when Bonn insisted on including West Berlin in the energy network.

I first explained my plan for a special economic zone to Foreign Minister Eduard Shevardnadze in the spring of 1988 and then to Premier Ryzhkov a short time later. They were both taken aback by my brashness. We could talk about it someday, they said, but the time was not yet right. Nevertheless, the idea of a special zone has been hotly debated in Moscow since the summer of 1989.

In the course of the Soviet decentralization of responsibility, citizens in the Kaliningrad region have formed certain organizations to prevent their area from becoming a permanent military province at the extreme northwestern end of the Soviet Union. These people are looking forward to the commercial use of the naval base of Kaliningrad once disarmament agreements have been signed. Since this port is ice-free and geographically convenient, they hope to turn it into a nexus of East-West cooperation. The neighboring Scandinavian countries have made the following suggestion (which would also apply following German reunification): After years of confrontation, the Baltic Sea could become an inland sea of intense economic activity, providing the impetus for the further development of the surrounding East and Middle European nations.

In any case, the growing self-assurance of the active groups in the Kaliningrad community is impressive. These mostly Russian citizens, who were born here after the war, are grasping the opportunity to give this region new duties and an identity of its own. They are seeking international cooperation, especially with the Germans. Unlike their parents, the postwar generation in Kaliningrad has no bitterness toward the German past of this section of East Prussia.

In this context, let me add a few remarks about the ethnic Germans in the Soviet Union. During the war Stalin scattered them to nearly all parts of this vast country, but proposals have recently been voiced for resettling these groups in the formerly German territory around Kaliningrad. Aside from the possibility that such efforts might be misconstrued as a nonviolent re-Germanizing movement, the Soviet Germans do not really wish to go there because they have no ties whatsoever to the area. Of the more than 2 million Soviet Germans, over 1 million are Volga Germans who are demanding the restoration of their autonomous republic and their repatriation to the areas from which they were expelled in 1941. On November 28, 1989, a resolution was passed by the Supreme Soviet; on December 25, 1989, the Soviet Council of Ministers set up a commission to establish the prerequisites for the autonomy of the old Volga area and for the repatriation of the former population. Nevertheless, these ethnic Germans, who are ready to leave, are quickly losing hope. It has become clear that the autonomous Volga German republic will probably never be reinstated, and no compensation will be made for the humiliating treatment inflicted by Stalin.

This is a bitter pill for the Soviet Germans who have served Russia loyally for generations, preferring to stay there in humane circumstances rather than return to their German homeland. The debates are still in progress, and it remains to be seen whether the Kaliningrad region would be a viable alternative. We cannot rule out the possibility that the Russians living there might welcome the Germans, who are respected as models of efficiency and hard work.

As for making Kaliningrad an industrial zone: The Soviet agencies dealing with this issue largely believe that a solid foundation for this plan has already been established. However, so much political energy is now being concentrated on the urgent problems caused by the current Baltic restructuring that Kaliningrad has been postponed. Nevertheless, among the possibilities viewed as feasible are joint ventures and also cautiously developed collaborations between Western firms and firms in the Kaliningrad region. All overland routes to Kaliningrad pass through Lithuania or Poland—two regions that are already casting greedy eyes at this Soviet enclave, with the result that the Russians living there are intent on developing this area on their own terms and using their own judgment.

In May 1990 I received an official invitation from the mayor of Kaliningrad to visit his city. His offer was preceded by my talks in Moscow with representatives of this region and the appropriate agencies of the central government. Having always been a restricted military zone, Kaliningrad is still not open to tourists without special permission. In mid-July, after obtaining a permit, I flew there by way of Moscow, accompanied by a small delegation from Deutsche Bank. The land route, as a glance at a map reveals, would have taken us through the (still) Soviet regions of Lithuania and Poland; there is no direct access to Kaliningrad from the Russian Federation even though the latter is politically responsible for that city. Shortly before our visit, the parliament of the Russian Federation had instructed Kaliningrad and other cities to begin preparing for their transformation into special economic zones.

Forty-five years earlier I had been wounded here, and a coal freighter converted to an emergency hospital ship had carried me to Copenhagen via Bornholm. Now, upon seeing Kaliningrad, I was profoundly moved. A great many things had changed. The cathedral, once the center of the historic part of town, was now a skeletal ruin; it was hard for me to find my bearings since all the other architectural signs of the once beautiful city had been eliminated. As a result the cathedral was virtually a memorial; it looms forlorn on the shore of the Pregel River, which flows through Kaliningrad from a now empty countryside. Immanuel Kant's stone tomb can be found at the rear wall of the cathedral, fully preserved under a protective roof. We stood in front of it lost in thought. And then one of our Russian hosts said that after four and a half decades it was high time we achieved a reconciliation in the universal spirit of Immanuel Kant, a great thinker venerated by Russians and Germans alike. Since Kaliningrad is planning a Kant Institute, I suggested that its opening be scheduled for June 22, 1991, the fiftieth anniversary of the German invasion of Russia. Let the place where Russians and Germans inflicted so much suffering on each other point the way toward a new future!

But back to my own glimpses of secret Soviet regions, which included not only Murmansk and a few other restricted military zones in that gigantic country but also the Baikonur space center, to which only one other Westerner, a statesman, was subsequently invited. As far back as 1986, the Soviets invited me to visit their famous Kosmodrome in distant Kazakhstan. They obviously wanted to inform me on the spot about the possibilities of commercial and/or scientific space travel by Westerners using Soviet rockets. Naturally I was excited by the offer, but I did not feel that the time was ripe for this sort of cooperation. The West German populace was worried, even frightened by the threat of Soviet SS-20 missiles, because Moscow was expanding their launching pads in its Asian areas. My visit could have turned the situation around by showing that the threat could be transformed into a peaceful joint use of space by Germans and Russians. The idea was enticing but problematic. The Soviets understood and accepted my qualms but hoped that they could soon provide a demonstration of reliable and meticulously functioning space services—especially given the prospect of German contracts and hard German marks.

I discussed the visit with Bonn; then, in late 1987, we agreed that in March 1988 I would attend the lift-off of a commercial launch vehicle at the Baikonur launching pad. This time my guide was Alexander Dunayev, head of Glavkosmos, a government institution responsible for the civil use of space travel. An experienced "fixer," he had developed quite a routine in his job after many years of attending these missile launchings. My hosts went to great pains to organize a special flight for me and my entourage that included a television crew and several German reporters.

I had insisted on having this contingent to forestall even the least suspicion that I was going behind Washington's back to get information about Soviet space research. The Americans, who had not yet recovered from the shock of the Challenger disaster in January 1986, were wary of our contacts with Moscow. I had learned how deep their mistrust lay when I happened to be visiting the State Department at the time of the accident in order to discuss our working with the Soviets.

However, shortly before leaving for the Asiatic republic, which is a long way from Moscow, we still did not know whether the reporters would be coming with us. The delay was caused by the usual turf squabbles in Moscow. At last Foreign Minister Shevardnadze, who asked to see me on the day before takeoff, gave us the final okay.

I was also assigned a top-ranking escort: German Stepanovich Titov, a three-star air force general in full uniform, whom I liked right away. He has since become the senior astronaut in the long line of space travelers whom the Soviets have sent into orbit. At the start of the 1960s he was trained with Yuri Gagarin, the first cosmonaut; then, as second test pilot, Titov achieved success in August 1961.

Guided by this veteran astronaut, who now holds the title of Hero of the Soviet Union, we visited the training center in Baikonur. We saw the practical but modest log cabins in which technicians and scientists prepare the cosmonauts for their flight. Titov showed us the narrow cot on which he and Gagarin had lain squeezed together for their "sleep test hours," while instruments recorded and evaluated any changes in their body positions.

Yuri Gagarin's historic maiden voyage took place on April 12, 1961. The Soviet Union outflew the United States by a nose. It was not until February 1962 that the first American, John Glenn, succeeded in orbiting the earth. (Glenn subsequently went into politics and today is a senator from Ohio.) At that time, when I was a young exchange banker on Wall Street, I watched the jubilation and the ticker tape parade. And now I was in Baikonur, standing next to Glenn's charming Soviet rival and listening to his tales about the pioneer days of Soviet space travel. General Titov proudly pointed to his chest and the multicolored ribbons signifying the medals he had been awarded, and he showed me an album of photos of his White House visit at the invitation of John F. Kennedy.

We were standing on the observation platform, just a few hundred yards from the launching pad of the Soviet Vostok rocket. As we watched the final preparations, an unexpected snow flurry swept between us and the huge spacecraft. We had been joined by an Indian delegation since the rocket was supposed to send the first Indian satellite into the cosmos to execute measurements of the subcontinent. We stood around Dunayev, the head of Glavkosmos, waiting and asking questions: Would lift-off be postponed because of the sudden bad weather? Dunayev was unflappable; he explained that some ninety-seven percent of all Soviet rocket launchings had been successful. And anyway, because of the split-second calculations of the orbit, a takeoff could be delayed for thirty seconds at the most. Even as he spoke we heard the preliminary roars of the rocket, which zoomed off punctually despite the snowstorm. We applauded. The Indian ambassador to Moscow, who had also witnessed the lift-off, promptly vanished into the nearby mobile transmission unit to notify his government that the operation was a success.

After the launching we were shown the jumbo hangars in which the space vehicles were assembled and equipped for new tasks. Sometime earlier I had seen the impressive and expensive NASA facilities in Houston, Texas, and I was now amazed at the simplicity of the Soviet installations here in Baikonur. General Titov must have read my mind, for he said almost humbly: "We can cope only with what we understand." He explained that these rockets had been designed for one-time use; on the basis of the first intercontinental missiles, they had been constructed as sturdy freight carriers with increasingly powerful engines. Components that demonstrated their value would be consistently improved to meet greater challenges.

The Soviets had clearly discarded their reticence toward the West. Dunayev revealed an amazing wealth of details. A proficient businessman, he answered all our questions about deadlines and prices; for example, if a Western firm were to put in an order, the product would be delivered by 1990–91. Furthermore, the Soviets would be willing to include a West German astronaut in a Soviet crew flying, say, a scientific mission. An appropriate laboratory at a Soviet space station could be rented for $15,000 per cargo kilogram, which would include the cost of transportation. In the summer of 1990 it was announced that a German astronaut would join the 1992 flight to the space station.

We will have to wait and see if these prices allow the Soviets to compete commercially with NASA or European Ariane Espace in this highly promising field. It would be a welcome development because we have been trying for a long time to get the Soviets to discontinue their backward form of international barter and move toward commercial exchange, with the emphasis on technologically developed products and on the services described above. Naturally, we cannot rule out the possibility of dumping, since no Westerners—and perhaps not even the Soviets—have a handle on how these prices are calculated.

Finally, we were shown something special in Baikonur: a joint satellite for exploring Mars. The first task of this thirteen-country venture was to probe Phobos, one of the two moons of Mars. West Germany was also quietly involved through the German Research Society. The project, under Soviet leadership, began in 1988.

The scientific head of the Mars project is Professor Roald Sagdeyev (who in February 1990 married Susan Eisenhower, the granddaughter of Dwight D. Eisenhower). After my visit in Baikonur, I met with Sagdeyev at his institute on the outskirts of Moscow, where he briefed me on this research mission. Sagdeyev, who is proud of being the only Soviet scientist in the Max Planck Society, explained to me that the Mars probe is the first space research truly worthy of the name. They were faced, he said, with interplanetary distances of over 120 million miles, whereas the orbital flight of the Baikonur rocket was a mere 180-mile jaunt from the earth's surface.

My question about the scientific purpose of exploring Mars led to a detailed trading of opinions about basic issues of man and the cosmos. For instance, they were anxious to know if Phobos, in the earliest geophysical times, had broken away from Mars or been drawn to it. Not altogether satisfied with Sagdeyev's answer, I kept inquiring, and I learned that another goal of the project was to track down the ultimate origins of mankind on this earth. After a long discussion I asked what inferences they would draw if they found no answer, whereupon the Soviet scientist spontaneously and loudly exclaimed, "Well, then I'll have to ask God!"

The Soviets failed in their elaborate attempt to investigate Phobos. Neither of the two satellites launched in Baikonur during July 1988 reached its destination. ESA, the European Space Authority, was involved in equipping the probes. In any case, Phobos 2, costing almost $500 million, managed to shoot photographs of the Martian moon from a distance of 90 million miles and transmit them back to earth. Supposedly they are of a higher quality than the best pictures taken so far by an American probe.

13·UNCERTAINTY AMONG OUR ALLIES

In the 1970s, when the United States was already keeping an eye on our loan talks with the Soviet Union, the American stance was what I would describe as "aloof attentiveness." In 1981, however, at the beginning of the Reagan era, they had a change of heart. I have already mentioned what Caspar Weinberger, the United States secretary of defense, said about the Polish debt situation; his talk of a "credit weapon" caused quite a stir. Soon Alexander Haig, the new secretary of state, also proved quite critical of our Eastern European contacts, and presumably Reagan agreed with him. During his first press conference after taking office, the president repeated the aggressively anti-Soviet statements he had often made during his tenure as governor of California.

This period coincided with the final phase of our Yamal pipeline talks, which involved several European allies (loans and equipment in exchange for natural gas). From the beginning the United States made accusations against West Germany and the participating firms since the negotiations were conducted privately. The charges were nothing new. We were accused of enriching the Soviet war chest with valuable Western currency, courting danger by becoming overly dependent on Moscow for indispensable fuel supplies, and weakening NATO both politically and militarily.

In the spring of 1982, I learned that President Reagan, at Alexander Haig's suggestion, wanted to send a special delegation of high-ranking government officials to Europe. Headed by Under Secretary of State James Buckley, they would ask critical questions of those negotiating with Moscow. These delegates, I was told, represented various departments and government agencies, not only the Department of State but also the Departments of Defense, Commerce, and the Treasury, plus the National Security Council. Well, we had to wait because the delegates were awaiting the go-ahead from the White House.

As sole representative of a private concern, I was asked if I would be willing to answer questions. I agreed, being sure of my position, but also aware that they would try to make me sweat.

Our meeting was scheduled for a Sunday afternoon at the American embassy in the Bad Godesberg suburb of Bonn. The Americans had landed in Frankfurt that morning, and their talks with representatives of the West German government were to begin in Bonn on Monday. I arrived punctually at the embassy, where I was taken up to the conference room. I asked my embassy escort about the ratio of hard-liners and soft-liners in the group. Gaping at me, he replied, "Soft-liners? They're all hard-liners!" So, before entering the room I knew what mood I'd find.

I sat down opposite seven men in dark suits; they looked me over with serious expressions. Evidently they wanted to go through a dry run for their government talks the next day, while their meeting with me was, of course, noncommittal. The intense questioning more or less dwelled on the standard charges. I felt as if I were hearing prefabricated and rehearsed formulas. When I finally was allowed to make a statement, I reviewed the historical background of our talks with the Soviets, the centuries of interaction between Russians and Germans, and my own observations and experiences during my frequent travels in that country. From the response of the men from Washington I could sense that they were not familiar with the special problems of a divided Germany and the overall European situation in the Cold War. I described our country's central position in Europe's historical development, which had embroiled us more than any other nation in the strife and tensions of this continent. I emphasized that from our perspective we could not resign ourselves to the present situation in Europe. By expanding our business ties we hoped to make a modest contribution to a very difficult and lengthy process of easing tensions.

From their American point of view, I went on, they should bear in mind that they were judging the behavior of their allies from across the ocean at a safe distance of thousands of miles, while the Germans knew that Soviet tanks were held in readiness positions a mere two hundred miles from the Rhine, ready to charge. We Germans could not ignore this threat, but it had no bearing on our loyalty to our alliance with the United States. The Federal Republic of Germany was, I strongly emphasized, a reliable ally.

When I closed the conference room door behind me, I could not tell whether my arguments carried any weight with those very self-assured delegates. I had somehow gleaned that they viewed me as a symbolic figure because of all my years as a critically observed leader of credit negotiations with the Soviet Union.

Since the issue of West German allegiance to the United States had been raised over and over again, I never took the matter lightly. The Americans were relatively calm, however; their fears were never as intense as those of some of our European neighbors, who suffer from a latent Tauroggen complex.* I have sensed this with the French who are normally open-minded and friendly toward us. The Americans, who know less about European history, often take us to task for being "too soft on the Russians."

* Within European memory the name Tauroggen recalls the German break with its Western neighbors in establishing an alliance with Russia. In December of 1812 in the small East Prussian village of Tauroggen, Count Ludwig von Yorck, commander of the Prussian troops fighting under Napoleon, decided—against the orders of King Wilhelm of Prussia—to withdraw his support of the French emperor. On December 30, 1812, the count signed a neutrality pact with Russia.

They strike me as being uninformed rather than intentionally nasty. Consequently I go out of my way whenever possible, especially in Washington, to do something about our most important ally's lack of knowledge.

As I have already mentioned, I was helped by my good rapport with Malcolm Baldridge, Reagan's secretary of commerce. We always respected each other no matter how divergent our opinions, which stood me in good stead when we came to a major hurdle in German-American relations: the so-called COCOM list. As the Soviet Union's biggest Western trading partner, we West Germans were particularly upset about that list, but so were other Western countries.

For years I attended no meeting in Moscow at which the Soviets failed to vent their anger at this list. At times they even lodged formal protests. They viewed the list as discriminatory and bluntly told us that as an independent nation we ought to get out from under America's thumb. During an official visit to Bonn in January 1988, Soviet Foreign Minister Shevardnadze spoke to a representative group of German businessmen. Without hesitation he told them how incensed his government was about the American embargo on exporting technology that had a military relevance. His frankness ("the damn COCOM list") was revealing. We understood the need for restricting exports of unequivocally military items or items that might have a military use as long as the Warsaw Pact existed in its current form, but we had always been frustrated because the list of prohibitions was inordinately long and contained no precise data about the possible military application of a specific commodity. As a result, some observers could not help feeling that the wording was deliberately convoluted and that the goal was to handicap European exporters trying to build up a commerce with the Soviet Union.

All these problems were on my mind when I flew to Washington. Besides meeting with people at the Department of Commerce, I had a chance to discuss some ideas with Professor William L. Stearman, a member of the National Security Council, and Jack Matlock, later an American ambassador to Moscow. Bill Stearman and I had several conversations that lasted for hours. This elderly, wise expert had been adviser to five American presidents. His experiences with Europe had expanded over decades, and his knowledge of history was extraordinary. He had good reasons for considering himself a hard-liner in regard to the Soviet Union, which often made it difficult for me to argue with him. But this did not prevent us from agreeing that the long-lasting tensions between East and West could and must be dismantled prudently, cautiously, and very gradually. Later on I heard that Professor Stearman kept the White House posted about our meetings.

When Gorbachev took over the Kremlin in the spring of 1985, Washington became more interested in the changes that could be expected in Soviet policy. The Americans, I observed, were at first extremely wary and hesitant, with good reason. In the past they frequently received détente signals from the Kremlin when it was faced with an acute emergency; but the fundamental tensions had never been relaxed, and no easing of the military threat to the West could be inferred from those signals. In short, as curious as Washington was about the new man in the Kremlin, its skepticism was stronger.

In early 1986, I got together with Under Secretary of State for Economic Affairs W. Allen Wallis at the State Department, whom I had met on earlier occasions. I told him about my experiences with the new team that was only just shaping up in Moscow. Once again I realized how intense and deep-rooted the anxieties of the two superpowers were. A short time later I met John O. (Jack) Koehler, a presidential adviser. He had been thoroughly briefed about my observations in the "new" Moscow and my first detailed conversation with Gorbachev. Through Koehler I met Charles Wick, a confidant of Ronald Reagan's. Wick, as director of the United States Information Agency, was in the process of establishing the International Advisory Council. I was asked to join this group, which was made up of equal numbers of media people and businessmen from all over the Western world. Their goal was to provide the United States administration with an unvarnished picture of the effects of its policies and to work out recommendations for Western leaders.

Our discussions were monopolized by Gorbachev's personality and politics. I learned firsthand how the various Western nations felt about Gorbachev and what effect the new Moscow policies had on them. I also took advantage of our talks to add my own experiences and observations to the opinion-forming process.

In the late summer of 1987, Washington was preparing to receive Mikhail Gorbachev on his first visit to the headquarters of the Western world. By then Jack Koehler and I had grown closer in our talks. He suggested that I send the president a brief memo outlining my views on Gorbachev's position and attitude in Moscow's policies. I accepted with pleasure. During a meeting of the newly created International Advisory Council, Ronald and Nancy Reagan invited us to a luncheon at the White House. I sat at the president's table, and he thanked me for my memo. Despite his early invectives about the "evil empire," Ronald Reagan, much to my astonishment, was open and relaxed in preparing for his meeting with Mikhail Gorbachev.

At a later White House function, in June 1988, I sat next to Nancy Reagan. Her mind was still teeming with her memories of their trip to Moscow in late May. The first lady, who was very down to earth and chatty, vividly described her impressions of the people she had seen in the streets of Moscow. She had visited a Soviet writer in Peredelkino, a suburban artist's colony and where Pasternak lived and is buried. Afterward, as she was heading toward her car, a couple of women from the neighborhood walked up to her without interference from the Secret Service men. Handing her a small bouquet, they said, "Mrs. Reagan, please tell us: Is there going to be a war between the United States and the Soviet Union?"

Nancy Reagan, recalling the incident, said, "I quickly pulled myself together, thanked them for the flowers, and said, 'My husband and I have come here to prevent war.' "

I could tell how deeply moved she had been by this small incident on the periphery of the grand events.

The world press had run sensational stories claiming that the two first ladies, Nancy Reagan and Raisa Gorbachev, did not initially get along well, and there had been tensions between them. I would have liked to ask Mrs. Reagan if there was any truth to those reports, but I did not wish to appear indiscreet. Nevertheless, I observed certain similarities between her and Mrs. Gorbachev.

I had had an opportunity to converse with the Soviet first lady in February 1987 at the Moscow Peace Conference and also in June 1989 when she and her husband were on an official visit in Bonn. I found her to be intelligent and clever, and I gladly admit that I was charmed by her. But no matter how much the two first ladies may have differed in background and education, I had no doubts whatsoever about their strong personalities and their influence on the two most powerful statesmen in the world.

After that first face-to-face meeting between Reagan and Gorbachev, Washington grew noticeably less distrustful about our talks in Moscow. The flow of information was smoother, and the two sides stayed in constant touch. But in retrospect I cannot deny that I spent many years operating in and suffering from the difficult tensions between Moscow and Washington.

Nor was it always easy to find a sympathetic ear in Bonn. This was hardly surprising, given the overall political climate of those years. While the politicians waited, tentatively eyeing one another, we bankers on a parallel track developed increasingly stable relations with Moscow. And since our Soviet partners, in keeping with the political structure of their country, were always government officials and not just businessmen, we were forced onto a terrain that was normally reserved for politics. This aspect, as I have repeatedly pointed out, did not exactly make our jobs any easier.

From the very start, however, I always stayed with my basic

outlook and acted consistently toward all three sides. I went by the principle that the Federal Republic of Germany is a reliable member of the Western alliance, but because of its central position in Europe, it has to have room—especially economic latitude—concerning Eastern Europe. I derive a certain satisfaction from knowing that we have made gradual advances in this direction and are now on the right path.

The resistance we came up against was not only in the public area. Because of my negotiations in the Soviet Union, I had to put up with occasional reproaches from friends—and even from my own family. Let me give you an amusing example. After the disaster at the Chernobyl nuclear reactor in late April 1986, I received an agitated call from my daughter who was attending the University of Munich. One has to understand the tremendous exasperation and uncertainty experienced by Western Europeans at that time. Occasionally their reactions verged on panic since almost no one could accurately gauge the possible long-term damage to human reproduction and to agricultural products. In the middle of talking to fellow students about the alarming news from the East, my daughter phoned me and snapped, "Your Gorbachev has inflicted this catastrophe on us!" After all, she said, I had become acquainted with him, had had a long talk with him, and had concluded that this general secretary was different from his predecessors and that we might have a chance for a real détente. And now this immeasurable calamity! "And there's no word from Gorbachev!"

Indeed, we were all dumbfounded and at a loss to understand why it had taken the Soviet government almost three weeks to come out with a plausible explanation for the planet's worst nuclear disaster. Glasnost and perestroika were still in their infancy. But I was unable to get any information that would help the West—and my daughter.

14 · DÉTENTE IN A DIFFERENT GUISE

Because of my many links with Moscow, I had to keep in almost constant touch with the Soviet embassy in Bonn. Good relations had to be cultivated on both sides because each trip's formalities and the agenda topics had to be carefully worked out in advance. After returning home I would often have talks at the embassy, recapitulating and explaining my experiences. Soviet ambassadors to Bonn are always meticulously hand-picked by Moscow, I feel, indicating how important West Germany is to the Soviets.

As I set down these memoirs, I can look back at my good, often friendly relations with four Soviet ambassadors on the Rhine. During the late sixties when I was getting ready for my first trip to Moscow, the Soviet ambassador to Bonn was Semyon Zarapkin. His tenure coincided with the passage from Chancellor Kurt-Georg Kiesinger's "great coalition" to Willy Brandt's social-liberal regime. That was the period of the so-called Eastern agreements, the core of which was the Moscow Agreement concluded in August 1970 by Willy Brandt and Leonid Brezhnev. This pact cleared the way for similar ventures aimed at lowering tensions with other Warsaw Pact members. I did not always have an easy time with Zarapkin, who unfortunately spoke no German but managed to get by in English. Still, he was an adroit and experienced diplomat with a certain Russian sense of humor, and so we ultimately managed to communicate.

He was succeeded by Valentin Falin, a man of a very special caliber. Until 1978 he had many opportunities to demonstrate his extraordinary skills. Endowed with a towering intellect and a thorough knowledge of the German language and German history, he quickly grew familiar with the various regions of West Germany. Falin had a lasting impact on German public life, and the numerous contacts he made are still valuable for both sides. In the course of our many talks, I admired his sharp mind and his polished debating skills. He was not easily flustered.

After the signing of the Helsinki Accords in August 1975, I asked Falin about Moscow's domestic application of the so-called Basket III, which concerns the protection of human rights in the thirty-five signatory nations. Given my experiences, I could not imagine, say, a free exchange of people and information, for this would involve opening the western Soviet borders. Aside from an infinitesimal number of exceptions, the average Soviet citizen had never been allowed to travel abroad or get information from foreign countries. By the same token, visitors arriving from the capitalist world were accustomed to being thoroughly searched— like suspected drug dealers. Falin dodged the issue with a masterpiece of dialectics: What the Soviet citizen needs or does not need or, more precisely, does not *yet* need—in terms of the "evolutionary" provisions of the Helsinki Accords—is a long-lasting process contingent on numerous facts and imponderables; this, however, does not prevent the Soviet Union from implementing the Helsinki Accords' provisions in every way. I listened carefully, but he must have sensed that I was not convinced.

Shortly before Falin returned to Moscow in 1978, we had a final conversation in which we summed up more than seven years of sharing ideas about our joint tasks. Thoughtful, almost melancholy, he told me how both moving and challenging his mission in our country had been. Since I went to Moscow almost regularly in those days, we agreed to stay in touch, and we later met frequently. He had joined a kind of brain trust set up by the Central Committee to deal with foreign relations. The brain trust also included Leonid Zamyatin, a future ambassador to London, and Mr. Portugalov: During the sixties Portugalov, one of the Kremlin's finest experts on Germany, had served at the Soviet embassy in Bonn.

In Moscow, Falin did not strike me as being all that happy. His mood changed under Gorbachev when he became head of Novosti, the Soviet news agency, which is so important in the exchange of information with other countries. In the fall of 1988, Falin succeeded Alexander Dobrynin as head of the Central Committee's International Division.

Dobrynin also impressed me as sophisticated and skillful at languages and also extremely important for the shaping of opinions in Moscow. He was vested with extensive powers, and prior to taking over the International Division of the Central Committee, he spent more than twenty years as his country's ambassador to Washington.

I understand that the job of heading the International Division has been slightly downgraded after the Dobrynin era. Nevertheless, I find it significant that by appointing Falin, the Soviets have replaced a diplomat experienced in the American realm with one having special knowledge of and experience in West Germany. Falin remains a vital link for us in Moscow, where his relations with West Germany are greatly appreciated. He has become known to a broad German public as an adroit media person, which in Moscow has earned him the reputation of being Germany's "complaint department."

In Bonn, Falin was followed in 1978 by Vladimir Semyonov, who has often been mentioned in this book. He certainly belonged to the "old guard" and to Moscow's solid stock of experienced professional diplomats. Having served as deputy foreign minister, he had a wide network of contacts throughout the Moscow administration. In 1982, Brezhnev was succeeded by Andropov, a capable politician bent on reforms. Semyonov, who was obviously familiar with him and had often told me about him, was visibly relieved that Andropov had become head of state. Like many other people, Semyonov expected him to enact many important changes. His grief and frustration must have been great when Andropov died prematurely after a far-too-brief term of office.

I followed Semyonov's career for many years: As an official government representative, he was extremely conscientious about his role in defending Moscow's interests, often in extremely precarious situations—for instance, when Soviet troops marched into Afghanistan or when the West German parliament decided to allow Pershing missiles to be pointed at his country.

Our countless meetings brought me many new insights and ideas. As I have said, we never lost our mutual respect even in the most trying and contentious situations. After Semyonov's departure from Bonn, we stayed on good terms, meeting on various occasions in both the Soviet Union and West Germany.

Meanwhile, Eduard Shevardnadze had become the supreme boss of the Soviet diplomats. The change in political style and substance was obvious on a personal level when he replaced Foreign Minister Andrei Gromyko. I had observed Gromyko several times during his visits in Bonn, both when he was alone and when he accompanied General Secretary Brezhnev. For me, Gromyko was living proof that deliberate confrontation and flaunting of power were the bedrock of Soviet foreign policy. I had only one opportunity to speak with Gromyko—at Gymnich Castle during a banquet given in his honor by the West German government. He struck me as having little interest in and probably scant knowledge of economics. I sensed that he was made uncomfortable by questions in this area, and therefore he could not be expected to sympathize with, much less supply incentive for, our economic cooperation.

At roughly the same time a perhaps trivial, but in my eyes characteristic, incident occurred in New York when President Reagan addressed the opening session of the United Nations General Assembly. His topic was world peace. That was the period, mind you, when both superpowers were stridently blaming each other for feeding international tensions. All at once, in his inimitable and effective way, President Reagan paused. His interruption seemed unexpected but had no doubt been carefully planned. Addressing Andrei Gromyko directly, he said in an easygoing tone of voice: "Mr. Gromyko, you are sitting here in front of us, very close to American Secretary of State [George] Shultz, only two rows behind you. If you turn around, you can easily shake his hand. Why don't we talk with one another!" The TV camera switched between close-ups of President Reagan's relaxed face and Gromyko's withdrawn, somber scowl. The blood had obviously shot to his head, and his Slavic features were tightly clenched. He offered no hint, much less a gesture, of compromise, nor could anyone who had known him during almost three decades have expected him to act otherwise. For years Gromyko was a dependable *nyet* man—which was a sign of predictability, albeit negative.

But now he was replaced by Eduard Shevardnadze, a native of Soviet Georgia. I had long noticed that in Moscow, the various Soviet ethnic groups seemed proportionately represented in high government positions. For us foreigners this added some welcome color, especially because of those from the southern republics, to the often monotonous and uniform tableau. We sober-sided Northern Europeans may have a similar response when encountering representatives of Southern European countries—say, in the Common Market. However, one cannot necessarily generalize. After all, Iosif Vissarionovich Dzhugashvili, the Jesuit student who changed his name to Stalin, came from Tiflis, which meant he was a southerner like Shevardnadze. And yet two different men could not be imagined.

Shevardnadze, fully in keeping with Gorbachev's aims, has been hard at work trying to smooth out the recognized distortions that have been plaguing Soviet foreign policy since the Stalin era. In our talks Shevardnadze, unlike Gromyko, has impressed us with his thorough background in and commitment to economics. This is hardly surprising since, as we know, the Soviet economy is a shambles, and solutions to the most vital supply problems have become test cases for the overall reform process.

In a country run by centralized planning, it was basically assumed that business and politics were inseparable, and so a more intense economic cooperation would indirectly influence political action. This is obvious in certain priorities established by Gorbachev. I have also been involved in situations, however, in which critical political developments had an adverse effect on sound business contacts.

A glaring example occurred in 1983 when Bonn was debating the NATO decision to set up American Pershing missiles on West German soil. Semyonov, the Soviet ambassador, lost no opportunity in asking me to intervene, pressing me, in a firm, if conciliatory manner, to talk my government into refusing the bases. He reminded me of the many years I had spent trying to improve our relations and managing to achieve more extensive economic agreements. But now he said he had to make it clear to me that further successes would be impossible if Bonn went along with the NATO decision. Our conversation took place on the eve of the Pershing debate in the West German parliament; the dramatic picture Semyonov evoked was on specific orders, no doubt.

Now and then such conduct may have created an unpleasant mood, interfering with relations that were normally level-headed and businesslike, but I must say that at no time in the twenty years of my dealings with the Soviets were our relations ever severed. Neither side gave the other the silent treatment; we never once even cold-shouldered each other. Thanks to our personal contacts, we always kept finding ways of continuing to talk—albeit sometimes in a less agreeable atmosphere.

In the spring of 1986, Yuli Kvizinsky began his mission in Bonn. We had to wait a while because he was still in Geneva as head Soviet negotiator at the talks on reducing intermediate-range missiles. Kvizinsky's predecessor, Vladimir Semyonov, had been in Geneva as Soviet negotiator at the SALT I talks on reducing strategic systems; and now, after years of frustration over the absence of concrete results, Gorbachev was anxious to reach a breakthrough in regard to the second major weapons category.

Kvizinksy's American counterpart was Paul Nitze. The two men became famous because of their frequently cited stroll in the woods when they supposedly reached a settlement, an event that startled the whole Western world. A play with the terse title *A Walk in the Woods* became a hit in New York and London.

In April 1990, Mr. Kvizinsky and I attended a German staging of the play *Der Waldspaziergang* at the Kammerspiele in Düsseldorf. Kvizinsky was very impressed by the actors.

One striking thing about Yuli Kvizinsky is his incredible knowledge of German, which he perfected as a young interpreter in East Berlin. We had long hours of highly productive conversations, and never once did I catch him making a grammatical mistake.

By the time he finally arrived in Bonn, during May 1986, still enjoying his aura as the "stroller in the woods," the Chernobyl disaster had only just occurred. Gorbachev had come to power a year earlier, but despite the new thinking, the Soviet Union behaved as it had always done in regard to such catastrophes. We learned nothing—at least nothing concrete; Moscow tried to hush up the incident or trivialize it. Charges were leveled not at the culprit but at others, including West Germany.

All at once I was faced with a terrible dilemma. As chairman of the joint German-Soviet Commission for Financial Matters, I was preparing for the annual meeting scheduled to take place in Kiev, of all places—a bare sixty miles from Chernobyl! We knew that a devastating wave of radioactive fallout from the exploding reactor had billowed across Kiev. Since the Soviets were still not informing us about the disaster, we received worried inquiries from our German delegates and from some of their wives wanting to know whether I intended to travel to the contaminated area despite what had happened. Through the representative of my bank I asked our Moscow counterparts to obtain a declaration from the International Atomic Energy Authority in Vienna that the Kiev area was absolutely safe. Otherwise, I told them, I could not assume responsibility for letting the West German delegates convene in Kiev.

Moscow stonewalled our expressed concerns. After all, they said, I had picked Kiev myself. They had agreed to my earlier suggestions of Munich and Stuttgart, putting their faith in my security measures despite the dangers posed by the presence of anti-Soviet exiles and agitators in those two cities. The authorities of the Ukrainian capital had already taken all the necessary steps to assure a smooth and risk-free conference. The chairman of the Kiev region had even scheduled a boat trip on the Dnieper for the German delegation.

Meanwhile, we kept receiving more and more horror bulletins from Kiev about the spreading contamination. Because of the prevailing winds right after the catastrophe, the Scandinavian countries and then Bavaria were affected by radiation before the Kiev area was covered by the direct fallout. In response to my inquiries to Moscow's West German embassy and the Foreign Office in Bonn, I was advised against going to Kiev.

Meanwhile the tone of our talks with Moscow became more and more irritated and exasperated. I reminded them that I had suggested Kiev as our conference site a year earlier when no one could have foreseen any disaster; but my argument fell on deaf ears. Yet I myself would have loved to visit Kiev. I couldn't reveal my real reason, of course. As a soldier I had gotten only a hazy glimpse of the Ukrainian capital in the late summer of 1941: German armored troops had just crossed the Dnieper to the south, and then, taking a wide eastern loop, they were encircling the city behind Semyon Budyenny's army. Back then Kiev did not yet have gold domes. What we saw were drab, gray onion domes.

Now, after Chernobyl, I finally gave up all hope of coming to terms with my Soviet interlocutors, whom I had already known for more than ten years. Hypersensitive egos and concern about the prestige of Kiev made an unbiased discussion impossible. But now I learned that Kvizinsky, the new Soviet ambassador, had arrived in Bonn. I offered to go and see him. He replied that he would pay me his first official visit.

During our long and productive luncheon conversation, I got to know a highly educated and skillful diplomat. When I broached the controversial issue of our planned trip to Kiev, I put my cards on the table. I told Kvizinsky that by insisting we adhere to the scheduled date and place, Moscow was making a dreadful mistake because safety concerns were preventing my delegates from going to Kiev at this time. The Soviet position was bound to have a negative effect on our previous cooperation. I suggested that we wait for things to calm down and that we reschedule our conference for that autumn and at a more remote location, with no publicity. If we could work it out, there would be no official cancellation, and nobody would be embarrassed. Every German participant would be notified personally and not in writing.

Mr. Kvizinsky's reaction was extremely reasonable. He indicated that in the next few days he would be attending a conference Gorbachev was convening in Moscow. This would be the first time that all Soviet ambassadors to Western countries were to be briefed about Chernobyl and its consequences. On this occasion he would settle our problem. And indeed he did. The negotiating climate improved tangibly, and the Soviets stopped their abusive behavior toward West Germany.

Having come to terms, we postponed the meeting of the Commission for Financial Matters, selecting Baku in Azerbaijan as the new site. This city, too, revived my memories of the terrible war. Shortly before the start of the Russian campaign in June 1941, when we were stationed on the Bug River, Baku had become a magic word in Nazi propaganda. Our government was trying to rationalize the sudden massing of Wehrmacht units on the German-Soviet demarcation line. We were told that Stalin was allowing our troops to march peacefully through southern Russia. The destination of our hazardous enterprise was Baku, on the Caspian Sea, and our goal was to join the Red Army in fending off a possible British attack. Now, decades later, I would indeed travel to Baku, but in a peaceful way.

Owing to Kvizinsky's intervention in the spring of 1986 a political and psychological deadlock was overcome. And this was merely a taste of the negotiating skill the Soviet ambassador frequently evinced during his mission in Bonn. At times great demands were made on him by the increasingly complex relations of our two countries, especially in regard to economic collaboration. Originally the new ambassador was not necessarily an economic expert, but when joint ventures were being discussed and the concomitant issues grew more and more important, he quickly became knowledgeable about the individual problems. He soon became an indispensable participant whenever we dealt with controversial cases. Kvizinsky's solid and discreet relationship with the Kremlin often proved very helpful to us.

It was announced in the early summer of 1989 that Kvizinsky, a confidant of Mikhail Gorbachev's, had been appointed to the newly overhauled Central Committee of the Soviet Communist Party. This meant that the ambassador's tenure in Bonn would be shorter than that of his predecessors—a development I regretted because of our mutual interests. In May 1990, Kvizinsky became a deputy Soviet foreign minister with a special mandate for the two-plus-four talks on German reunification to be negotiated between the two Germanys and the four major World War II Allies (the U.S., the Soviet Union, Great Britain, and France). I consider his absence from Bonn a loss, but it is also a welcome fact that a man with his proven expertise on the German situation is working in Moscow. In view of his background, he will do a fine job of representing his country's interests as an experienced if not easy negotiator at the two-plus-four talks.

His successor in Bonn is Vladislav Petrovich Terekhov. Having once served on the staff of the Soviet embassy in Bonn, the new ambassador already knows our country and our language. I am certain that we can continue our long-standing essential and constructive dialogue.

A critical investigation into Soviet foreign policy from Stalin to Brezhnev had already begun right after Gorbachev took office. Since 1985 one central task of the Soviet reformers has been a comprehensive stock-taking and analysis; the conclusions are to be applied to the future image that the Soviet Union wishes to project abroad.

I had a chance to gain some personal impressions from talks with several competent men, especially Valentin Falin, V. V. Sagladin, Venyamin F. Yakovlev, and V. I. Dazhichev. The latter two are professors of history with the necessary detachment from current events, and they also fought in the war as I did. All four of these men advise the general secretary in different areas. The results of their investigations, which I learned during conversations with them, could be summed up as follows:

At the start of the Stalin era, the Soviet Union, greatly weakened by war and revolution, initially focused on building up a clear-cut military power vis-à-vis the West. All resources, both human and natural, were ruthlessly channeled toward this end. Top priority was given to heavy industry and the armaments industry. The rulers neglected the standard of living for the broad masses, and in pursuit of their goals they were willing to provoke the West, sometimes deliberately. After 1945 the wartime alliance soon degenerated into confrontation, chiefly because of the issue of how to treat a defeated Germany. The Cold War and the rapid escalation of mutual threats triggered an arms race of unforeseen proportions. NATO and the Warsaw Pact emerged as "defense and offense" alliances.

During one conversation I casually mentioned that Joseph Stalin deserved a posthumous Order of Merit from NATO because if not for him, NATO would never have been created in the first place. No one contradicted me. Even in the 1970s when the Moscow-Bonn treaty helped to ease tensions, the Soviets kept up their side of the arms race to the point of positioning SS-20 missiles. But now they had gone too far. A phase of Western indifference, accompanied by Moscow's incessant protestations of peace, came to an end. This new and so far most serious threat could not go unanswered. The West, partly at the insistence of West German Chancellor Helmut Schmidt, set up its Pershings.

During that period the West was also irritated by Soviet expansionism. Surpassing the expansionist traditions of the Czars, Russia reached far beyond continental Europe to Africa, Central America, and Central Asia. Afghanistan was the last straw. The West finally woke up.

The Soviet Union has reached the limits of its capabilities on all sides. Also, looking at history, we cannot possibly brand the Soviet Union as the only country guilty of expansionism. For centuries Europe has always given military policy precedence over the social welfare of its citizens. The minister of war has always been the top man in the cabinet and has translated foreign policies into action. Expansion has usually been the supreme European goal. A war had to be won; and if it was lost, all financial resources were drained to do a better job of preparing for the next war. A vicious circle evolved, and for a long time it had no chance of being broken. But the future promises to be different, even in the minds of the Soviet rulers.

The twentieth century has proved that global wars can no longer be waged. They solve no problems but only create new ones. This realization came at a high price—some 60 million corpses. Karl von Clausewitz, the Prussian philosopher, described war as a continuation of politics by other means, but his statement has become obsolete. All Europeans must face the new situation.

Those, briefly, were the thoughts of my Soviet interlocutors on the earlier foreign policies of their country. However, their critical survey of the past is not being hailed universally. Protests are coming not only from government officials but also from private citizens, especially the older generation. How can a centuries-old attitude about nation and fatherland, for which vast numbers of people suffered during the Great Patriotic War, have suddenly lost its validity? This offends the patriotic sensibilities of many Soviets, and these sensibilities are being taxed to the utmost by a press that takes its cue from glasnost. I have been told about lawsuits brought against journalists for "fouling their own nest."

On the other hand, the population has generally sympathized with Gorbachev for terminating the war in Afghanistan. Having no direct connection to this Soviet "Vietnam," he could readily bring the soldiers home without embarrassment. His action revealed his extraordinary strength of will. He ended this nightmare of steadily rising casualties in a war that was not patriotic, sparing his generals an inglorious retreat and helping the Soviet economy.

An improved economy was also the goal when Gorbachev tried to straighten out the Soviet relationship with the other Marxist superpower: China. Military tensions are gone from the eighteen-hundred-mile border between the two countries, although the Soviet Union still has a deep-seated fear that an overpopulated China might someday invade the unpopulated vacuum of Siberia. The Soviet Union will always keep its military presence on the Chinese border, but Gorbachev's visit to the People's Republic of China in May 1989 at least eliminated the vestiges of an excessive distrust.

The Soviet Union has recognized that after decades of threats, more is to be gained from a policy of negotiation and cooperation. The first elements of this new insight were discernible in Gorbachev's visit to West Germany in June 1989.

A great deal of mistrust toward Moscow's "charm offensive" had to be overcome. For the time being, however, I felt it was advisable for NATO and the Warsaw Pact to continue as frameworks for helping to keep order in Europe. These two alliance systems can provide military and political safeguards during the risk-free transition period when the arsenals are being gradually dismantled. Even if the two sides were ultimately to reach a plateau of equal security or a "structural inability for mutual attack'' (I doubt whether this is possible in military practice), NATO, to my mind, would still have its legitimacy. Anyone who expects or demands the termination of NATO fails to see that the Western defense alliance is based on a system of shared values. Thus, NATO is first and foremost a natural union of countries with similar convictions and only secondarily an alliance in the classical sense, to ward off an acute threat. When NATO was founded, it was accompanied by the wish that these pact systems would sooner or later become superfluous.

I concur with my Soviet interlocutors: The foreign policy of the future will be *to establish new priorities as tensions are eased.* Such new priorities would include the fostering of human relations as well as economy and ecology in their interrelationship, science and technology, culture, sports, and exchange of visitors. These notions are already spelled out within the framework of the Soviet-German Declaration of June 30, 1989. Now they have to be acted upon.

15 · ENCOUNTERS WITH OSTRACIZED ART

It became clearer and clearer to me during my travels that the Soviet Union contains not only tremendous material resources but also spiritual treasures that command attention of the same magnitude. Beyond my many business talks and negotiations, I had a number of unexpected experiences during the 1970s. One of the most exciting was my encounter with the art of this country—specifically, Russian avant-garde painting. This movement, which began around 1910, included such artists as Marc Chagall and Vassily Kandinsky as well as El Lissitzky and Kasimir Malevich, the founder of Suprematism, about whom, like the Soviets themselves, I had only the haziest awareness. When Stalin seized power after Lenin's death, the avant-garde artists were abruptly outlawed and shrouded in oblivion—at least in their native land. Now all at once I was confronted with solid evidence of that creative era.

By a fortunate coincidence I happened to make the acquaintance of Georgi Costakis, a Russian of Greek descent who was on the staff of Moscow's Canadian embassy. After the last war he launched into a search for paintings, objects, collages, gouaches, watercolors, and drawings from that period. His tremendous energy was matched by his luck. He put together the finest private art collection to be found—unofficially—in the Soviet Union. Its highlights were the great and renowned names in Constructivism and Suprematism, two original and typically Russian schools. Costakis's apartment—his private museum—was located in a high rise on the outskirts of Moscow. His address, known only to a chosen few, was a secret carefully guarded by connoisseurs and museum curators.

Costakis had grown distrustful after a number of threats and burglaries. It was not easy to gain admission to his small but—by Moscow standards—baronial home. Visiting him was a delightful relief for me after often strenuous negotiations. Moscow evenings were dreary, and once you had the unavoidable Bolshoi and the circus behind you, other possibilities of entertainment were rather meager. You quickly got tired of the hotel bars, which accepted only foreign currency, thus excluding the Muscovites (who nevertheless, drawn by curiosity, flattened their noses against the windows). So I welcomed those hours in Costakis's apartment.

Evenings here were cozy, we were like a family. Our intensive viewings of art, which were endless because of the hundreds of objects, were interrupted when Mamuchka Costakis served tea and a wonderful apple cake. The apartment was so jammed and cluttered with pictures and objects that we had to observe extreme caution while viewing because we risked catching a heel in a painting on the floor—perhaps one by Alexander Rodchenko or Olga Rosanova. Costakis gave us the background of every artist and every picture.

Lively and precisely he described a whole era of Russian painting whose creativity and dynamism certainly made it second to none in importance and expressive power. The impetus of this era was probably the shock of the Revolution of 1905, which, although abortive, continued to smolder, carrying the sparks of the events of 1917. I was fascinated by the idealism of the young avant-garde artists who wanted to radically change the morbid fin-de-siècle society. Thus, for a while, the avant-garde and revolution went hand in hand.

I was struck by the surprisingly large number of female artists: Alexandra Exter, Natalya Goncharova, Nina Kogan, Lyubov Popova, Nadyezhda Udolzova, to name just a few. Despite their single-minded goal of explosively reshaping the world, they remained self-assured and independent, with no emancipatory posturing. They and their male colleagues later influenced the Bauhaus, de Stijl, and Dada movements, and even developments in Paris, the largest center of art between the two world wars, and then New York after World War II.

One day Costakis confided to me that he wanted to return to Greece, the land of his forebears. But he intended to leave a good three-quarters of his paintings in Russia, the country of their creators. He wanted to take along only a small number, but this would require help from the West. He had been relying on Edward Kennedy, whose large autographed photo was prominently displayed in Costakis's apartment.

After Costakis revealed his plans to me, I noticed that he had become nervous and restless. Now that he knew the value of his collection he was less happy about his pictures and lived in constant fear of their being stolen. Also, his children thought he should sell them. The Soviet government agreed to house the collection in a separate wing of the huge Tretyakov Gallery. (After a long delay and the expansion of the museum, the rooms slated for the Costakis collection are scheduled to open in the near future.)

Since time was obviously running out, Costakis asked me to help him get an exhibition in Düsseldorf or Cologne. That would be the Western debut for the paintings that he wanted to take along—over two hundred. He could give me only three days to arrange a show. I had long felt that this unique offer was well worth any effort and expense, but I hadn't reckoned with the cumbersome arrangements that had to be made with our official West German cultural representatives. Only after great struggles and bitter disappointments did I manage to keep my promise and my deadline.

The paintings were cleaned, framed, and hung, and in September 1977, just before the opening, they were previewed on television. My friend was beside himself with joy. For many years he had lived with the paintings—some uncleaned, all unframed, stacked up and jumbled together in his tiny Moscow apartment. And now he saw them in their full glory, free of any conspiratorial atmosphere and on display for a sophisticated and critical audience. Tall, heavy, and every inch a southern European, he kept hugging and kissing me in joy and gratitude.

The exhibition at the Düsseldorf Art Museum was an unexpected triumph for Costakis. He was tumultuously celebrated by an international audience and by art dealers and museum directors from London, New York, and Tokyo. He stood amid his paintings and the many visitors from all over the world, seemingly intoxicated by the many unfamiliar impressions. A hangover was inevitable.

Since then, his exhibition has traveled to all major art centers. As for Georgi Costakis, he evidently had a hard time coping with life outside Russia, and I tend to doubt that he found any inner peace. Costakis died in the spring of 1990. Efforts were then made to sell parts of his collection.

Meanwhile, word had gotten around in the appropriate Moscow circles that I was interested in Russian and Soviet Russian art, so now I was receiving and accepting more and more invitations from unofficial and unapproved artists, with whom I also made contact in other ways. While my official counterparts seldom invited me to their homes (probably because of their modest housing conditions), the artists never hesitated to invite me. These get-togethers in an artist's or sculptor's studio or apartment were to me the most personal and most productive encounters in the Soviet Union. I got to know a very modest but extremely pleasant milieu in which I felt immediately comfortable. I also found sizable apartments and studios on a par with Western standards.

One artist who did not have to be embarrassed about his surroundings was Ilya Glasunov, who has now become known in the West. He can be described as a true pet of the Moscow art guild, although not uncontroversial. Glasunov, who has painted nearly all the great leaders and likes to focus on historic figures and places of national Russian significance, continues to be hailed. His works, usually shown at important places, draw record crowds. He spurns abstraction and Constructivism, and thereby the now classical paintings of the avant-garde that I have been discussing.

In Vadim Sidur, a sculptor who also paints, I met a very special breed of artist. Shortly before the end of World War II, half his lower jaw was shattered by a German bullet. When this former Red Army soldier and I got together in his basement studio, the full absurdity of our wartime experiences erupted once again.

Sidur is known as the Russian Henry Moore. His sculptures have been world-famous for a long time even though he was blacklisted for some time in his native land. In 1968 he hailed the Prague Spring as a "rejection of a dehumanizing ideology." In 1987, Sidur was posthumously rehabilitated, clearly at the instigation of Boris Yeltsin, then mayor of Moscow, and a major retrospective of his work was presented in the Russian capital. After Yeltsin's removal from office, the exhibition was closed. When I tried to see the show in the spring of 1988, I learned about the details of its cancellation from Sidur's widow, an extraordinary woman who had stood by her sensitive husband with all her strength. I then wrote a letter to one of the Soviet negotiators, Minister of Culture Sakharov, informing him of how disappointed I was that this exhibition was no longer on view. I told him that I hoped I could visit it during my next stay in Moscow. My letter was successful.

I had long nurtured a wish to co-organize cultural projects with the Soviets in addition to large-scale business deals. I felt that such cultural undertakings held the promise of being a positive force in fostering mutual understanding. Art exhibitions struck me as one of the most appropriate possibilities.

In 1981, Moscow's Pushkin Museum opened a rich exhibition entitled *Moscow-Paris*, paralleling the *Paris-Moscow* show held a year earlier at the Centre Pompidou in Paris. The Soviet show was attended by the Party bigwigs, who were given wide media coverage. The press ran a photo of Leonid Brezhnev standing in front of a large well-known Matisse painting. He was quoted as saying: "Art is an excellent way to promote mutual understanding."

Grabbing the newspaper, I took it to the Ministry of Culture where, pointing out the Brezhnev quote, I proposed an exchange of art exhibitions between our two countries. The minister of culture was Dementsev, a member of the politburo, and his two deputies were F. W. Saitsev and C. P. Popov. At first they were astounded to hear this suggestion from a financier, and they asked me whether I was sure I was in the right office. But I insisted and so they listened. After several meetings between the Soviet Ministry of Culture and Deutsche Bank, a private institution, an agreement was reached on co-sponsoring an exchange of art exhibitions.

The timing was right because we were just completing our anything-but-simple Yamal pipeline negotiations, which the Soviets hailed as "the deal of the century." A significant event like the first steps toward an exchange of art shows was appropriate. From the very outset our bank participated in the art talks and assisted in the overall organizing. Art experts were on the job on both sides, and over the years they developed a close personal rapport with one another, which helped in the arrangements for several shows in Germany and the Soviet Union.

Man and Landscape, the first Moscow exhibition of contemporary German art, was organized and supervised by the Rhenish-Westphalian Art Society in Düsseldorf. On March 18, 1983, I opened the exhibit with my fellow negotiator, the deputy minister of the Soviet Ministry of Culture.

There is another reason why that date is fixed in my mind. That morning, together with the leaders of the City of Moscow and the head of the municipal authorities with whom we had negotiated, we laid the cornerstone for our building, which was to house our Moscow office. By now, we had outgrown our rooms at the old-fashioned but otherwise very pleasant Hotel Metropol. We had therefore made the following suggestion about a small and once beautiful structure in the old part of the city: We would rebuild and restore this now decrepit building and use it for our purposes. On the day of the foundation ceremony, we completely forgot our arduous efforts to obtain a building permit, the long obstacle course all the way up to the Soviet Council of Ministers. At last we had a place of our own.

The exhibition opening, which was scheduled for that evening, remained up in the air until the very last moment. An overzealous official at the Soviet Foreign Ministry took issue with our carefully prepared catalog, which indicated that a large number of our artists were in West Berlin. We were told that since ours was an exhibition of the Federal Republic of Germany, we could not include Berliners: There were "Federal Republic Germans," "GDR Germans," and, as a distinct third category, Berliners. It was purely owing to the perseverance of our Moscow ambassador, Dr. Andreas Meyer-Landhut, that a compromise was worked out just in time. The Russian text in the bilingual catalog was revised, but the German text remained intact.

The opening was a dazzling affair. The entire Moscow art world had been invited—an unprecedented occurrence—and they turned out almost in full force. I was told that this was the Soviet capital's very first exhibition of contemporary Western painting. When the Muscovites gathered at the opening, you could tell by their faces, their appearance, and their behavior that each one was an individualist with a truly artistic nature. Normally you would have had great difficulty meeting any of them.

I went through the exhibition with my Soviet colleague, offering elucidations and hearing opinions. Soon somebody pointed out to me that we were being followed and listened to by many of the generally young guests—all of them potential artists. It made me feel like the Pied Piper of Hamelin. I recognized a few of these people; I had met them while enjoying the Moscow art scene in basements, catacombs, garrets, and back alleys, and we had discussed their work. During my earliest visits I had queasily sensed that I was arousing false hopes. Some of them must have assumed I would be helping them gain recognition in the West so that they could finally escape the ghetto of their semi-underground existence in the Soviet Union. All too often I had noticed that my interest in their art and my questions about their daily lives triggered unrealistic expectations. I considered this tragic for both sides.

The reader ought to know about the moral dilemmas facing a Soviet artist. He has only two choices: Join the Society of Artists of the Soviet Union, with its twenty-two thousand registered members, or else go his own way more or less as a loner and outlaw. Membership in the society entitles the artist to a modest stipend, and he is allowed to participate in official exhibits and publish catalogs. The nonregistered artist, being denied such opportunities, has to fend for himself. I noticed that some of them managed to get along by selling their works to foreigners, especially diplomats, but most of the "unofficials" barely managed to eke out a wretched and undignified existence. Yet what preys on their minds is not so much their material plight as their lack of recognition as artists.

In the mid-sixties a loosening of the virtual quarantine seemed about to ease their dismal situation. But then, in the early seventies, this trend was abruptly terminated when some nonconformist artists held an unofficial exhibition at a building site on the edge of Moscow. Using bulldozers, the city police closed down the show. The government announced that there was only one artistic style: Socialist Realism. The Moscow artists and also the Western public saw this as a brutal return to what they considered outmoded dogmas. The result was profound dismay. I must add that the officially sanctioned art has also produced quite respectable works. Quality can be high or low on either side.

One last remark on our first Moscow exhibition of Western art (1983). Despite its huge success I must concede that we may have put too great a demand on the Soviet viewers. In their first exposure to contemporary West German art, they were certainly very receptive and curious, but given their traditional backgrounds in art and their lack of comparative standards, some of them suffered a culture shock. We learned about this from notes left in the suggestion box, which we had prudently set up to gauge responses. Their recurrent leitmotiv was astonishment at the basic pessimism of many works, which did not fit with the Soviet image of life in the Golden West.

This exhibition was a breakthrough. Moscow reciprocated in December 1984 in Düsseldorf when the Soviet Ministry of Culture mounted a rich exhibition covering several centuries. Presenting a new picture of Soviet art, it drew a great deal of attention. The show was accompanied by a panel discussion at which experts on both sides engaged in a frank exchange of views. Gorbachev had not yet come to office, but the event already showed that such a platform offered the artists a chance for better mutual understanding despite ideological misgivings in both camps.

Our positive experience encouraged us to tackle a project that would take a long time to carry out: *War and Peace*, a joint exhibition of works by Soviet and German artists who, having personally experienced the horrors of our century, were able to portray and excoriate them and also the plague of earlier periods: war. The focus of the exhibition would be on the two wars between Germans and Russians in the twentieth century. This would be linked to a warning that a new and even more brutal conflict would make survival hopeless for either side.

The theme was certainly a challenge. Would the cooperation we had been aiming at forestall controversy and mutual finger-pointing that could wipe out all our efforts? Or would the vow that such an outrage would never again be permitted be the more eloquent component in the paintings? I was rather skeptical in view of what I had already seen in museums, movies, and art books. Would we be reopening old wounds in the people who had experienced the war in Russia?

Before this exhibition became a reality in the winter of 1978–79, we sponsored a preview. During our visits to the west Siberian gas fields, we had been deeply impressed by the morale of the people laboring in this harsh climate. As a gesture of solidarity we brought a Horst Janssen show to Novosibirsk and then sent it on to Moscow. Horst Janssen, a brilliant sketch artist, has done a marvelous job of depicting Russians and their landscape, and his portraits of Russian writers and poets are very powerful. He also painted the excellent portrait of Tolstoy that Helmut Schmidt, the West German chancellor, presented to Leonid Brezhnev during the latter's visit in Bonn. On several occasions the general secretary's widow has lent us this portrait for exhibition purposes.

The *War and Peace* project took about three years to materialize—a time span consistent with its theme. At the request of the Soviets the title was changed to *Terror and Hope.* Selecting the works caused many headaches in both countries. To my delight I soon ascertained that the Soviets were excluding all propaganda and ideology.

At the Peace Congress in February 1987, I learned that for the first time in decades a "semi-official"—that is, tolerated—exhibition of nonregistered Soviet artists was to be mounted. Over sixty of them would be showing their works at a squalid site at the very edge of Moscow. A few of the artists were present, standing in an orderly line by their own pieces, their faces filled with expectation. Once again the news of my coming had spread. I was embarrassed because I could not fulfill their hopes for major purchases, but while viewing their works I realized that we could not open our joint exhibition six months later without including one or two of these paintings. I explained this to Minister of Culture Sakharov, and he agreed. His response was further proof that the old rigidity was slackening.

Ultimately the exhibition comprised three hundred works. In

October 1987 it was officially opened in Hamburg's Kunsthalle. The exhibition moved on to Munich where it was opened by Mayor Georg Kronawitter. Next, in the spring of 1988, Minister of Culture Sakharov and I led the opening ceremonies at Moscow's Tretyakov Gallery and then at Leningrad's Hermitage. It was late May, and this colorful city on the Gulf of Finland was in full splendor. Professor B. B. Piotrovski, renowned both at home and abroad as the doyen of Soviet museums, welcomed the guests warmly. The exhibition was a resounding success everywhere, far surpassing all our expectations.

Thus, I had discovered yet another hidden aspect of the Soviets, the art archipelago. My encounters—both official and semiofficial—with Soviet artists became one of my favorite pastimes. A whole human realm opened up here, far from my commercial and sometimes intense contacts in this country.

With each exhibition I had to get in touch with two high-ranking officials: the minister of culture and Professor Tair Salakhov, the first official secretary of the Association of Artists of the Soviet Union. A native of Baku, Azerbaijan, Salakhov, who has a great deal of southern charm, is an extraordinarily sensitive representative for his association. His wife is an attractive and widely admired prima ballerina, and he himself is a painter. He insisted on doing my portrait, and I sat for him in his modernly appointed Moscow studio. His charcoal drawing now hangs in my home as a souvenir of our frequent meetings during those years.

But there were some difficult times. In Moscow, Düsseldorf, or Frankfurt, when discussing our project with Tair Salakhov, the representative of "official" art, he would recommend his distinguished but of course registered, government-approved colleagues, while I was frequently thinking of the nonregistered artists who lived poorly and were not always able to find an audience. I had to be very tactful when bringing them up, but also I knew that my Soviet colleagues had long been aware of my forays into the art underground.

I had other unusual encounters. Involuntarily I became an

intermediary between Soviet artists and high Soviet officials who might otherwise have never had a chance to meet. I made a point of casually bringing together major representatives of the art world and people I knew from my business dealings. This added to my wealth of experiences. Frequently I invited museum directors to these gatherings—for instance, Professor Korolyov, head of the world-famous Tretyakov Gallery. I was astonished to discover that these people had never met.

In 1978, Falin left his post as ambassador to Bonn. By then the two of us had had very detailed exchanges of our ideas on art. I told him how surprised I was that the Soviet Union was depriving both its own population and foreign countries of the great works of the classical avant-garde artists. Why not use the upcoming 1980 Moscow Olympics to put an end to this stagnation? Following the example of the 1972 Munich "Olympiad of the Arts," they could offer an extensive retrospective of the Soviet avant-garde in addition to the athletic events. Falin, who was both open-minded and knowledgeable about that creative period, seemed very interested, but he gave me no definite answer. Stalin's denunciations were obviously still in effect.

I noticed this again at a later juncture. It was during the summer of 1982 in Leningrad when we signed the Yamal pipeline contract, which the Soviets praised highly. Feeling generous, they asked me if I had any special wish that they could fulfill in honor of this memorable occasion. I asked if I could view the (secret) treasures of the Russian avant-garde artists, which are stowed away in one of the most beautiful buildings in Leningrad, the Russian State Museum on the Square of the Arts. During the previous century, long before the revolution, this former city palace of Grand Duke Mikhail had been turned into a domicile for the arts, but the paintings I was interested in were not on display; they were locked in a storeroom like a kind of contaminated waste that had to be carefully walled up. Nevertheless, I got to see these magnificent treasures, which lay neglected in a dark cellar. The experience was unforgettable.

It took the government a long time to relax the restrictive art policy that it had maintained for decades. I sensed that this attitude was not the opinion of the individual art officials. They were quite open to the avant-garde, but none of them had the courage to support these "controlled substances."

An obvious change came about in the summer of 1988 when Sotheby's held an auction of contemporary Soviet Russian art. A decisive role in this event was played by Pavel Khoroshilov, head of the official sales bureau of the Artists' Association for Contemporary Art. This man, a former exhibition commissar at the ministry, had worked with us for years, preparing the shows that I have described in this chapter. The Sotheby's auction made us all feel as if we had been liberated from chains worn for many years. Mr. Khoroshilov's joy was not unimpaired, however; for him the true unshackling will come when the Soviet population develops a strong and well-founded interest in its avant-garde art. For now foreign buyers still dictate the events, causing more irritation than anything else. Soviet Russian painting has obviously become rather trendy in the West.

16 · THE BIG RECONSTRUCTION

On February 7, 1990, the Soviet Central Committee abolished the constitutional power monopoly of the Soviet Communist Party. The most important building block of the state, created after the October Revolution of 1917, was declared obsolete.

To grasp the full scope of this decision, one has to know the Communist Party's history and its central importance for the Soviet Union. Lenin, who founded this state, made sure that the Party retained all power. He established the authoritarian framework that, based on Marxism-Leninism, was considered the sole and infallible purveyor of truth. This new orthodoxy was designed to push transcendental concepts into the background and supplant all religion. Stalin knew how to exploit this ideology and the Central Committee to make the Party obedient to his will and to become dictator. (His despotism was viewed by the populace as similar to the absolutism of czarist days; and Stalin saw himself as the indirect descendant of Ivan IV, known as Ivan the Terrible).

Later on, under Khrushchev and Brezhnev, the gory atrocities stopped, but it was obvious even to a foreigner like myself that the Communist Party still controlled all nerve centers of power. The Party was the steering apparatus, and together with its bureaucracy, its presence could be clearly felt not only in the police and the army but also in the economy. The Communist Party was identified with the state as a matter of course, and no one would have dreamed of protesting. According to some people, its iron grip was necessary to hold together the republics and the more than one hundred national groups—in short, the gigantic hetero-geneity of the Soviet territory.

Eventually all the Communist states adopted this tyrannical system, voluntarily or under duress. Even the Chinese, who have a very different mentality, copied this intrinsically alien Party dictatorship. Mao Zedong spent over two years in Moscow as Stalin's guest and disciple. I have conversed with Soviet scholars who actually felt that Stalin deliberately placed an Asiatic stamp on his image as a ruthless dictator. This might explain why the Beijing leaders still venerate him as a shining example. The other Eastern bloc countries watched suspiciously when East Germany adopted the Marxist-Leninist principles. As the star pupil of the "Communist class," which so zealously and perfectionistically created a workers' and peasants' state, East Germany was not exactly popular.

In view of this central role of the Party, it is not surprising that for a long time Gorbachev, in the traditional need for power and control, could not imagine encroaching on the Party's power monopoly—even despite the demands voiced by opposition groups since 1988. I have already mentioned Gorbachev's school friend Zdeněk Mlynář. In his book *What Can Gorbachev Change?*, which was published in 1989, Mlynář postulates that notwithstanding the adverse ideas of opposing parties, a single political party (that is, the Communist Party) could qualitatively alter the system to be more democratic. This standpoint was advocated by Gorbachev until the spring of 1990. Why else would he have traveled to Vilnius in mid-January 1990 to dis-suade the Lithuanian Communist Party leaders from declaring their independence from the Central Party in Moscow.

While visiting Moscow in April 1990, I heard the view that Gorbachev had grossly misread the situation: In January 1990 it may still have been possible to agree on a more orderly procedure for channeling Lithuania's later separatist aspirations, but Gorbachev would have had to go along with the autonomy demands of Lithuania's Communist Party, especially since he could have gotten help from Algirdas Brasasuskas, a man enjoying authority and prestige among the local population.

Given all those events, the Soviets were amazed when Article 6 of the Constitution was eliminated in February 1990 (with the assent of General Secretary Gorbachev) and the power monopoly of the Communist Party was abolished.

Since then the Party's influence, taken for granted during more than two generations, has been pushed back with mind-boggling resoluteness. Change has been following change with breathtaking speed and with a magnitude that would have been called historic just a few years ago. In March 1990, Mikhail Gorbachev became the first elected president of the Soviet Union and was equipped with vast powers. As a result, the overall might shifted from the Communist Party to government institutions. The deliberate weakening of the Party's role was blatant. The presidential election was handled by two parliamentary institutions that are still learning how to practice democracy: the restructured Supreme Soviet and the Congress of People's Deputies. The politburo and the Central Committee of the Communist Party (the traditional power centers) were not involved—at least officially. A sixteen-member Presidential Council was created (the membership is now seventeen). Except for the chairman of the Council of Ministers, who has an ex officio seat and vote, all the members of the Presidential Council were handpicked by Gorbachev. According to several of its members who have explained its operations to me, this is not an executive organ. Nevertheless, before making important decisions, Gorbachev makes a point of seeking advice from the Council, which therefore has a de facto influence. The president's new governmental practices will lead to a curtailment in the traditional functions of not only the politburo but also the government itself, that is, the Council of Ministers.

No one denies that the example of the United States has played a major part in these changes, but the Soviet Union is still a long way from developing a democratic system resting on a separation of powers. Also, in contrast to the American model, the Soviet Union has a fully staffed executive corps with a premier and many, far too many ministers. For this current phase the Soviets may be imitating the system of the French Fifth Republic, which was created some twenty-five years ago by de Gaulle. In France a president invested with far-reaching powers shapes national policies, which the prime minister and the cabinet members have to follow. Nonetheless, after my observations and conversations in Moscow during the spring of 1990, I have no doubt that America's constitution and governmental makeup have had an impact on Moscow.

A propos, the powerful attraction exerted by the United States can also be felt in everyday Soviet life. This is demonstrated not only by the long lines outside McDonald's* and the unavoidable Pepsi sign, but also by the badly copied early morning TV shows. Of course, after so many years of deprivation, one can sympathize with the Soviet public's enthusiasm for a halfway exciting entertainment program. Still, we wonder if such amusements or abuses, which have long been familiar in the United States, might not damage the culture in this great, proud land and the positive sides of the "Russian psyche" (however that notion is interpreted).

But back to the Party. The twenty-eighth Party Congress, originally scheduled for October 1991, was moved forward to October

---

* Let me add a comment here. One of McDonald's best-known products is probably the Big Mac, whose greatest statistical advantage is one we can easily test: It is identical on all continents, since it is always based on the same recipe. It therefore constitutes an ideal standard for comparison for currency theorists, who would like to compare local currencies with one another and with the dollar. If one converts the 3.75 rubles charged for the Big Mac to the official rate, the price would come to $6.25 (whereas the comparable item in the United States costs $2.20). Naturally, the analysis could be repeated for a number of national currencies by using this "hamburger standard."

1990 and then July 2, 1990. This shows the urgent Soviet need to clear up the irritating conditions within the Party and its public stance. The Party was racked by harsh clashes between reformers and conservatives led by Gorbachev's adversary, Yegor Ligachov, an ex-member of the politburo. For months the most frequent word used in political discussions was *raskol,* meaning "split" or "dissidence." In its impact for the future, the twenty-eighth Party Congress was no less important than the twentieth in 1956 when Khrushchev launched de-Stalinization. Under Gorbachev's masterly aegis, the twenty-eighth Party Congress, superficially viewed, passed resolutions that supported him in every way. A qualified majority reelected him as general secretary and placed his personal candidate, Vladimir Ivashko, a Ukrainian described as rather bland, in the newly created position of deputy to the general secretary. Ligachov, Gorbachev's conservative rival, got nowhere; he was not even reelected to the freshly staffed politburo, a fate he shared with Premier Ryzhkov.

Boris Yeltsin's dramatic resignation from the Party at the end of the Congress made it obvious that Party conditions can by no means be viewed as peaceful and orderly. Gorbachev wants to "combine a broad democratization [inside the Party] with centralism and discipline," thereby inaugurating what his friend Mlynář has already indicated. But presumably they have only just begun to fight. Not only has *raskol* existed for a long time between the Party and the people, but it will continue plaguing the Party internally. A multiparty system can, at most, be delayed, but it cannot be stopped. New political groupings formed long ago, and they will evolve into new parties that describe themselves as social-democratic, Christian-democratic, or liberal. The question arises whether this movement toward pluralism, which, as in the other Eastern European states, challenges the very right of the Communist Party to exist, can proceed in a halfway orderly manner.

Finally, we must bear in mind that the two quasi-parliamentary bodies, the Supreme Soviet and the Congress of People's Deputies, still have a long way to go before accomplishing an efficient parliament that can handle and pass laws in a businesslike fashion. We can all too readily understand why the new officials are seizing opportunities, such as those offered by television, to speak publicly and create public images. But so far the results of the parliament have been quite paltry. A great deal of time is wasted because discipline and preliminary efforts within the caucuses and special committees are insufficient, and the frequent absence of expertise is matched by a general inexperience with parliamentary procedures. Still, despite these obvious inadequacies and contradictions, the positive changes made under the heading of "glasnost" are unmistakable for anyone familiar with the Soviet Union.

Perestroika, in contrast, was tackled only halfheartedly. The right concepts could have been implemented, but the courage was lacking. Gorbachev is well aware of this. While aiming at a détente in Soviet foreign policy, the "new thinking" has triggered previously unknown domestic problems, especially in regard to ethnic and social issues. Social changes can develop a dynamic of their own, however, and the overall effects defy prediction. For decades a brutal exercise of might created a passive immobilism that was buttressed by a mentality of forbearance and lethargy; this made the domestic political climate static, tranquil, and also predictable for Soviet rulers. But today, perestroika, the call for restructuring, demands a liberal view of society. As a result, the intentional creative ferment is inevitably linked with social outrages that are not unknown in the West.

17·THE ECONOMY IS STILL THE DECISIVE FACTOR

In April 1990, the thirty-five member states of the Conference on Security and Cooperation in Europe met in Bonn. The document they published at the end of their meeting came as a complete surprise. Although not a binding agreement, it indicates the direction for reshaping economy and society during the last decade of this century. The specific economic goals are the creation of basic requirements for a market economy, the right of private property, a price system free of government regulation, and the convertibility of currency. The specific political goals are a democratic multiparty system on the basis of free and secret elections, a constitutional state, and the observance of human rights.

The objectives of this declaration largely correspond to President Gorbachev's own intentions. But if I compare these goals with today's Soviet reality, I am forced to conclude that nearly all the planned changes are in opposition to the prevailing conditions. Gorbachev himself describes the imminent economic reform as his country's greatest turning point since the Revolution of 1917. And this change is desperately needed because so far the previous reforms have had little effect.

For years now, serious think tanks in the Soviet Union have been comparing the Soviet system with the Western ones and coming up with sophisticated analyses and conceptions. In this context we ought to single out IMEMO, the Institute for World Economy and International Relations. The overall impact of those think tanks, however, has been minimal. As in Western countries, an ongoing critical dialogue between the Soviet hierarchy and the practitioners is imperative if an ambitious program is to be carried out, or putting it more precisely, if a new Soviet Union is to be created. At the moment I am overwhelmed by the magnitude of the necessary measures.

President Gorbachev is not nurturing any false hopes. By the spring of 1990 he had been in office five years, but as honored and celebrated as he may be abroad, his domestic position has become more precarious. In the first six months of 1990 the Soviet supply situation was worse than ever—if not catastrophic. Now, after initiating only minor and halfhearted steps toward economic reform, the Soviet president, invested with extensive powers, has ordered radical action. The vice premier, Professor Leonid Abalkin, has been put in charge of this reform program. Nikolai Petrakov, a professor of economics and personal adviser to Gorbachev, is working on a plan that deliberately begins where Lenin's New Economic Policy (NEP) left off. After extensive discussions with Abalkin, Petrakov, and other members of Gorbachev's circle in April of 1990, my impression is that they are ready to launch severe measures that could be viewed as the "last resort."

At its first session the newly created Presidential Council was unable to reach a consensus that would have encouraged Gorbachev to put the population through a radical cure. While they are not denying the urgent need for reforms, the experts are worried that the required measures might falter at the halfway mark because Soviet citizens are completely inexperienced in the laws of the marketplace. The inefficient methods of operating during the past few years have reduced the prospects of success and make the efforts and actions needed for change seem even harder to obtain. In regard to implementing its reform policies, Moscow is having a more difficult time with its populace than the other East European governments; as Moscow struggles with the problem of the Soviet Union's enormous ethnic and cultural differences, it has no previous experiences as models.

Finally, in May 1990, after weeks of debating, the Presidential Council recommended a reform package to Gorbachev. One of its crucial points is the reduction of food subsidies; this would bring huge price rises because Soviet prices are completely out of synch with actual manufacturing costs. The 1990 national budget includes 96 billion rubles* for price subsidies, roughly twenty percent of the total budget. In the changeover to a market economy, prices must be adjusted and ultimately left to the free play of market forces. Premier Nikolai Ryzhkov, who linked his political fate to this reform package, has announced the news to the people. Expecting severe reactions, even violent demonstrations, the government is awaiting the results of a popular referendum—an innovation in this country and a sure sign of Moscow's insecurity. The procedure for carrying out this unusual step has not been made clear, however.

If we take a closer look at the Presidential Council's reform package, we note that despite all the promises of "radical" concepts, the measures seem as halfhearted as ever. From the very outset the government has aimed to incorporate a safety net for extreme cases of social hardship, but instead of allowing creativity and stressing self-reliance as an approach to success, the "regulated" market economy about to be launched reveals all too clearly the old pattern of a command economy.

Other negative factors are also present: a dangerous tendency to follow old formats and rigid hierarchies as well as the inertia that dates back to czarist times. How then can Moscow bolster the people's willingness to become more productive? The only way the motivation necessary for an efficient economy can be created

* In August of 1990, as this book goes to press, Soviet officials in the United States and elsewhere were unable to furnish a reliable rate for conversion of rubles to U.S. dollars. If we use the Big Mac as a standard of comparison (see footnote, p. 178), these 96 billion rubles, with a buying power of 25.6 billion Big Macs, convert to roughly $56 billion.

is by intensifying the individual's desire to make more money.

By way of example, the following story is making the rounds. When Gorbachev decreed that improved work would henceforth command higher pay, new salary guidelines were introduced. A Western TV correspondent stationed himself outside a factory in order to get verbal and visual responses to this news. Most of the responses were hesitant or negative. One woman's comment was typical: "I've always been able to relax and earn ninety rubles a week. Now I'm supposed to work hard and get one hundred rubles. No way!"

In talking about the "Russians," I am quite aware of how problematic generalizations are, especially since the "Russians" make up just about half of the Soviet population. Nevertheless, I feel that the habits that have prevailed over centuries plus the spiritual education in the Orthodox faith have made these people modest, patient, and inured to suffering. The resulting apathy cannot be overcome immediately. To put it in simple terms, efforts to do so can lead to passive resistance. This mentality along with social envy has probably engendered a hatred for cooperatives and for rudimentary private enterprise, both of which, despite occasionally controversial methods, are achieving a few successes.

The Chinese are frequently cited as proving the opposite. Their education has supposedly focused on worldly values. Twenty-five hundred years ago the teachings of Confucius emphasized the virtue of love for parents and clan, as well as justice and *success*, all of which created wider flexibility and greater willingness to take risks.

While these peculiarities of the Soviet situation are difficult to describe objectively, other problems can be more precisely defined and analyzed. One of them is the Soviet Union's credit standing, which has been deteriorating rapidly since the fall of 1989. A nation's credit worthiness in the international capital market must be understood as a criterion of assured autonomy; if a debtor is considered a good credit risk, he can choose his lenders and negotiate the best terms. Moscow needs a huge array of imports that have to be financed with hard currency borrowed from the West. But in contrast to the pre-1989 period, commercial loans amounting to many billions of dollars are no longer possible. What worries everyone is not so much the enormous volume of credit as the steep increase in debts within a short amount of time.

Two factors have triggered this decline in the credit situation. For one thing, because of the decentralization of responsibility, Soviet firms and collectives are now permitted to buy goods directly on credit, either by making use of deferred payments or else by taking out loans. However, the managers are not experienced with debts; they don't know how to take out and handle these loans, calculate the interest due, and make punctual payments even though they are now permitted to use any hard currency they have earned. By the same token, Western companies have no experience in dealing with the individual Soviet enterprise, which has just become independently involved in foreign trade.

So far the Soviet state itself has been responsible for paying all such debts through the government's Bank for Foreign Economic Affairs. Occasionally a payment may have been delayed, but it was always assured. This reliability gave Moscow a high credit rating. Over the past twenty years I have personally experienced the soundness of the Soviet credit rating over and over again, and I have always given positive replies to any questions about it.

Back in the mid-twenties the newly founded Soviet Union was already buying German machinery, which it financed with bills of exchange. German bankers had a saying: "Russian bills of exchange are as good as cash." During the subsequent decades, Moscow was as reliable as ever. But it must also be stated that the Soviet people had to suffer deprivation because repayment of loans took precedence over necessary imports. The government did not want to lose prestige by falling behind in its foreign debts.

Much has changed since 1989, and both sides have to get accustomed to the new situation. As the Soviets adopt a market economy, Westerners will also have to change their way of thinking.

The second factor that caused a decline in the Soviet credit rating has to do with Moscow's indebtedness, which during earlier decades remained within narrow margins—totaling at most $35 billion, nearly all backed by Soviet gold reserves. But for years now the price of gold has remained low, as have the prices of petroleum and natural gas; in fact, the prices of the main Soviet export items—all of them natural resources—have been depressed throughout the world. The situation was totally different after the 1973 oil crisis. From 1974 to 1984, in the pre-Gorbachev era, the prices of petroleum and natural gas escalated rapidly. As a result, the Soviet Union, being the world's largest producer of primary energy, took in higher amounts of Western currency than it had anticipated. Because of contracts signed during the seventies and early eighties, West Germany had to pay the largest share in these transactions. At one point, on the basis of my own observations, I calculated the increase in receipts during that period: $170 billion. But my Soviet counterparts corrected me; it was actually $200 billion.

We and the Soviets have long been wondering what became of those huge windfall profits. Westerners occasionally talk about a "Marshall Plan"—that is, huge loans to the Soviet Union. Imagine the reforms that could have been carried out with that windfall! Instead, the proceeds were consumed by armaments, the war in Afghanistan, and payments to Cuba, Vietnam, and the like. That money could have been spent on a structural overhaul of the obviously precarious Soviet economy, expenditures that would have involved neither interest rates nor repayments of debts.

Even at that time an urgent task was the improvement of the infrastructure: the transportation and telecommunication systems so indispensable to a modern economy. But Moscow missed its chance to install these fundamental needs for an economy based on a division of labor. The effects of these omissions have been disastrous. For instance, within the framework of the abovementioned agricultural consulting initiative, a coordinating committee made up of Soviet importers and foreign exporters as well as other specialists was supposed to devise a plan for the recovery of Soviet agriculture. From the very outset banks would have been involved in working out the overall plan by arranging special credit agreements to guarantee the eventual financing. This 1984 plan had the following priorities: to supply agricultural areas with a system of collection and transportation consisting partly of grain elevators and produce depots; and to set up refrigerated containers for shipping the perishables to consumer centers.

I understand that Gorbachev bitterly regrets this state of affairs and that his chief goal is to reduce a heavy industry and arms production. Germany will have to grant loans based on state credits to Moscow to support the Soviet restructuring process. In June 1990, West German banks lent Moscow 5 billion deutschmarks ($3 billion at the then-current rate of exchange), ninety percent of which is guaranteed by the West German government. This political move at that crucial time is enabling the Soviets to overcome the most immediate needs of their cash flow problem and to forestall further jeopardy to their credit rating. These sums, which are not earmarked for any specific purposes, will most likely be channeled toward debt payments to Western exporters. In the summer of 1990, Moscow owed 3.8 billion deutschmarks ($2.275 billion) to Western businesses, including 1.5 billion deutschmarks ($.892 billion) to German firms.

In the course of the initial negotiations on the forms of German reunification, the Soviets demanded billions in credits to make up for what they consider their material losses when East Germany moves from the socialist to the capitalist economic bloc. Added to this financial compensation is the cost of stationing Soviet troops in East Germany.

One of the structural weaknesses of the Soviet economy is the lack of medium-sized industries. Most of the factories are enormous but geared to a single product, and although concentrated in one area, they have to supply the whole of this gigantic country, so flexibility is out of the question. An entrepreneurial spirit was not requested and could not be developed even with the best of intentions. Furthermore, the confusion that has been mounting in the domestic situation of the Soviet Union since early 1990 is likewise damaging the Soviet credit rating.

To my mind, if Gorbachev's reform plans are ultimately to bear fruit, the most urgent focus of Western support efforts should be on advice and training. These goals have top priority even over credits. One has to learn how to make a sensible use of loans—that is, large amounts of currency. The squandering of hard currency is one of the greatest sins of the past.

Management training and consulting are indispensable to the handling of loans. But perhaps these sophisticated terms should not be used at present. The immediate task for the Soviets is to acquire the fundamental business accounting skills—to determine and calculate costs, for example. But such calculations are impossible as long as the unit cost of a product cannot be computed. What is the good of allowing factory managers to follow their own judgment in order to achieve greater efficiency if no basis exists? Unlike China, the Soviets cannot learn from earlier experiences because such knowledge was barely evident during the czarist era.

Many years ago I engaged in a lively discussion with planning officials who were looking for ways to launch systematic training. I tried to point out that if you are dealing with a person assigned to perform certain tasks, you cannot get him to practice "new thinking" by installing a new chip as you would in a computer. For many generations, I went on, the people functioned differently, and change can come only gradually, which presents a difficult timing problem for this gigantic country.

In the spring of 1988, when I was negotiating a 3-billion-mark loan with Premier Nikolai Ryzhkov, I was given clear indications that heavy industry was losing its priority and that strenuous efforts were being made to improve the overall supply situation. For the first time, loans were to be directed toward consumer goods, thereby upgrading the standard of living. These credit requests were inspired by the general reshuffling of Soviet economic priorities. Gorbachev's efforts to overhaul Soviet society and economy had been going on for three years, but the man in the street had seen no tangible results of perestroika. On the contrary: Even a foreign visitor noticed that in Moscow, which generally enjoys a far better supply situation than the provinces, the stores offered an increasingly smaller selection of goods, while some of the better items were simply unavailable.

Referring to these shortages, which I had personally witnessed, I told Ryzhkov that I viewed a lower standard of living as inevitable: The old stagnant economic system had been rejected, and the new one had not yet taken effect. Ryzhkov explained that the deutschmark loans would be used for purchasing capital goods for light industry, that is, the food industry and the consumer goods industry. The critical supply situation should be improved, he said, through greater efforts on the part of industry itself. He was certain that the investments would have an effect within a relatively short time: The output of consumer goods would lead to tangible improvements in the supply situation by late 1989.

The goals struck me as being too ambitious and the deadline too tight. I countered that the restructuring and modernizing of the Soviet economy would require a longer time span. Moscow would therefore have to keep the Soviet living standard on a satisfactory plateau by resorting to temporary consumer imports to prevent a supply crisis. These stopgap measures would be imperative until the demands for food and consumer goods could be met by the Soviets' own modernized industry.

Despite the directness and urgency of my remarks, my arguments got nowhere. Ryzhkov felt that valuable hard currency credits should not be spent on consumer goods; by producing no profit, this would dissipate the funds. Understandable as his position was, I could sense Moscow's anxieties about Soviet prestige: Consumer imports could be viewed as an obvious sign of weakness in the Soviet economy. The leaders feared that the Soviet

Union might be cast in the role of a developing country. Also, their worries may have been increased by the example of the final phase of the Khrushchev era.

I therefore submitted a conciliatory proposal to Ryzhkov, explaining it as an overall conception. My suggestion was that part of the loan be applied to modernizing their light industry and their consumer goods industry. The appropriate Soviet agencies should determine as quickly as possible which Soviet industries and companies could benefit from advice and modernization in order to establish ties with the appropriate German equipment manufacturers. Another part of the loan should be spent on immediate imports of consumer items. Once the production in modernized Soviet factories improved in both quantity and quality, consumer imports could be curtailed little by little and finally eliminated altogether. But Ryzhkov didn't like my conciliatory proposal. He remained adamant that Western loans should not be "frittered away" on consumables.

We were the first to offer credits for improving the lot of the Soviet people, but a short time later our Western neighbors— France, England, and Italy—offered loans to Moscow for similar purposes. The Soviets still have problems making sensible use of these credits. They have had to admit that earlier—and much smaller—loans were wasted on machines that then rusted away in some warehouses. In view of the large number of loans announced in the early summer of 1988, I had qualms about whether these problems could ever be solved by the current Soviet political and economic administration. I doubted whether Soviet consumer needs could be even halfway satisfied by the planned economic reforms; unfortunately, as it turns out, my skepticism was justified. Apparently the supply crisis, which might easily escalate into a social or even political crisis, can be overcome only if Soviet leaders resort to the quasi-emergency measure of importing consumer goods.

Granted, further loans would greatly increase Moscow's foreign debt. The great problem, of course, is not the slide in its credit standing but the Soviet inability to get imported consumables quickly and efficiently to the markets, that is, to the consumers.

Soviet distribution capacities are completely underdeveloped, an effective logistics is lacking, and throughout the distribution network there are skillful hands that slice off a bit of the pie long before it reaches the final consumer. This predicament became shockingly clear after the Armenian earthquake when the Western nations, in a spontaneous and generous effort to help, dispatched enormous amounts of supplies to the victims, even transporting these items to the stricken areas. This was the first time that glasnost fully revealed the plight of the population and that the Soviet Union accepted Western help without restrictions. Nevertheless, only a tiny fraction of the food, medical supplies, blankets, and clothing reached the needy. The bulk was lost because of carelessness or stockpiling in the wrong places. The more valuable items were siphoned off, not infrequently ending up in the hands of Moscow officials.

This bitter experience confirms any suspicion that a greater volume of consumer imports might not contribute to an improvement in the supply situation for the man in the street. Even in a time of horrifying emergency, a fast and efficient distribution broke down for a relatively small area with a low number of inhabitants. How then could it possibly succeed across this immense country with an enormous population that has been suffering the most elementary deprivation? As long as human and technical incapacity is mated with corruption, a quick end to the supply crisis appears unlikely, however great the effort. Willing as the West may be to support Moscow's reform struggles, the necessary decisions have to be made and carried out within the Soviet Union.

As far back as 1987, Mikhail Gorbachev encouraged the formation of cooperatives in order to get private enterprise under way. Their aim was to improve the supply situation of consumer goods. Starting off on a small scale, the commercial sector and the service sector—for example, cafés, restaurants, and newsstands—managed to activate the general supply system. The government initially praised this development, and the population made brisk use of the unusual array of commodities. The number of people employed more or less privately in the cooperatives soared from 70,000 in 1987 to 4.5 million in 1990. But customers soon realized that the prices here were higher than in the state shops. There was no comparison in quality, however; the wares in cooperatives were much better. There were instances of price-gouging in certain cooperatives that took advantage of the shortages and the lack of competition. The consumers felt cheated and called these "entrepreneurs" evil capitalist profiteers (after all, they had long since learned the vocabulary); they demanded that wrongdoers be punished. At times the resentment led to outbursts of physical violence and even worse. This profiteering is associated with free enterprise, and it therefore tends to discredit the market economy as a whole, which permitted such abuses in the first place.

Since I was personally intrigued by this debacle, I tried to get background information from the head of the Association of Cooperatives, Professor Vladimir A. Tikhonov (no relation to the former premier), who belongs to the Academy of Sciences and to the Congress of People's Deputies. It was not easy locating his headquarters, located in a sleazy part of the Soviet capital—an area I had never visited. When we finally found the address, I was concerned about going up to his office on the second floor because the building was still unfinished and appeared unsafe. I ventured inside even though I doubted it was the right place. Eight or ten young, muscle-bound men were outside the office door; in this unfinished stairwell, they looked more menacing than inviting. In response to my hesitation, I was told that these men were bodyguards. When I was eventually led into the office, I found myself in a very dimly lit, ramshackle space. I know you can't expect much when it comes to interior design in Moscow, but this was distinctly below the customary level.

I met not only the association president Tikhonov but also Vice President Goltsman and other members of their staff, who were all likable. The group reminded me of a painting I had seen at a museum in Rome showing an early Christian gathering in the catacombs. The countenance of these pioneers of a better life resembled the faces of conspirators: haggard, almost fanatical, and deeply committed. A smile would have been out of place. President Tikhonov gave me a detailed description of the successful development of the cooperatives, whose total sales in 1989 had zoomed to 40 billion rubles. But then he vehemently complained about the government's failure to help them or to protect them from physical threats. The need for bodyguards became evident. He also talked about the misconduct of several cooperative members. When he asked me for my opinion, I pointed out that it was the job of the association either to remove the troublemakers or to correct their behavior. The cooperatives, I said, were the spearhead of a market economy, a system tailored to the needs of the people, and they had every chance of being regarded someday as the pacesetters of the new era. It was no doubt misguided of them to defend abuses, and they would do better to be as open as possible in order to keep their members and their price policies above suspicion. Furthermore, it would be a tremendous help if they treated their customers in a friendly way, which was something Soviet consumers had never experienced. This minor episode shows how difficult it is to grasp the laws of the marketplace much less accept them as guidelines for one's own behavior.

Another huge task facing the Soviet Union is the conversion of the arms industry into factories for producing consumer goods. I discussed this problem with the director of the Commission for Conversion Affairs, Professor F. N. Avdiyevski, an influential member of the Academy of the Sciences, and Dr. Yuri Andreyev, whom I have known for a long time. They explained the desperate situation. These oversized armaments plants are government enterprises that manufacture civilian products only in exceptional cases. The same is true of their American counterparts, but they are noncentralized private companies, most of which also have technical and marketing experience with consumer goods. Notwithstanding the conversion obstacles that also exist in the West, the managers, who bear full responsibility for such firms, usually have the necessary flexibility and are not accustomed to relying on the government. Meanwhile, this issue has assumed crucial importance for the Soviet Union. This was made obvious during the spring of 1990 when a large number of Soviets participated in the International Exhibition of Conversion Affairs held in Munich.

There is an ongoing debate as to whether the East European nations, especially the Soviet Union, should be granted a kind of "Marshall Plan" aid in the form of generous credits to help them in their reconstruction. I have my doubts about this idea. There is no question that the Soviet supply situation, indeed the overall economy, is in a terrible, even dangerous condition. Some of the people dealing with the reforms are bombarded with stories about the mismanagement that is surfacing everywhere. Going beyond mere descriptions of the Soviet plight, these tales, almost by suggestion, have created an enthusiasm for meaningless manipulation of numbers. This has led to a tangle of proposed solutions. Yet in the Soviet Union, which may be the country most in need of economic reform, there have been few public statements concerning the "Marshall Plan." This diffidence should be respected! The other East European nations in the process of restructuring may be doing the right thing by choosing the "Marshall Plan" route. Throughout this vast and long-term restructuring of Europe, the Soviets, purely for political reasons, must maintain their capacity to act and their generally accepted influence as a major power. For our sake, too, the Soviet Union must assume a role within the international community seeking to maintain order and stability in global politics. Just think of China!

To fully grasp and judge the Soviet Union's special economic and social condition, we have to know a great deal about this country which finds itself in a situation that is like no other in the world. The Soviet predicament makes the problems attending the unification of East and West Germany seem minimal by comparison. Cash injections, as necessary as they may be, would by themselves be woefully inadequate in the Soviet Union. Cooperation in the broadest sense will be indispensable for a long time. Nevertheless, any solutions must bear the imprint of Soviet leadership.

When I discussed these matters with Professor Nikolai Petrakov, he disavowed a brief news item ascribed to him. It claimed that he did not rule out Western assistance in the form of a "Marshall Plan" to help in solving the economic crisis. Professor Petrakov stressed that Western aid, while vital to the Soviet economic program, had to be implemented on the basis of parity and cooperation between the partners. As I took leave of him, he added: "Respect our pride!"

I must also cite a particular conversation I had with Dr. Alexander N. Yakovlev, who was secretary of the Central Committee until the twenty-eighth Party Congress. Today this closest confidant of Gorbachev's is a member of the Presidential Council.* Dr. Yakovlev expressed it unequivocally when he highlighted the Soviet role as a superpower and a major factor in global order: "What we have to achieve will also benefit the West. We are not begging for charity." We must therefore ask what steps the Soviet leaders are taking in order to keep justifying this approach.

* In April 1990, Yakovlev left the Communist Party and thereby the Central Committee. As a member of the Presidential Council, he transferred to the Kremlin, taking over the function of the president's chief of staff—a position modeled after its American counterpart. Yakovlev's duties as secretary of the Central Committee of the Communist Party are now being performed by Valentin Falin, who was elected to the Central Committee where he is in charge of international affairs.

18 · THE NEW EUROPEAN ORDER AND THE SOVIET UNION

Many paths have led me to Russia during the last few decades—and to the writing of this book. In the course of this long time span, my motives have been as diverse as the prevailing atmosphere during my encounters with the Soviets. My conversations and impressions were accompanied by constant change. Things were not always friendly, and occasionally it seemed almost presumptuous to hope for better times. Setbacks in the climate lurked behind every appointment. The reasons were usually not to be found in my agenda topics or on the level of our talks. Most irritations were dictated by the prevailing international political climate. It is time to examine whether it was objective disagreement or mutual distrust, perhaps even simple misunderstandings, that led to political friction in East-West relations and caused a reciprocal hardening of positions.

All those things are now history. The Cold War chapter is finished, and it can be turned over to the historians. But what will follow? The two superpowers, the United States and the Soviet Union, have always given their relationship full precedence over all other political developments. What will become of this still somewhat tenuous relationship in the very near future?

A whole generation in both the East and the West has been shaped by this almost fateful enmity between the Soviets and the

Americans and Eastern and Western Europeans. Many people have experienced this hostility firsthand. In the course of nearly four decades the overall confrontation, though at times repressed, has penetrated the very depths of our minds.

New concepts are needed for the future, but reorientation is a difficult process. In early 1990, Lawrence S. Eagleburger, U.S. deputy secretary of state, shed a tear for the Cold War. With something like a deep, heartfelt sigh, he recalled that in those days the lines were sharply drawn and the camps neatly staked out, making the overall political situation a lot simpler and easier to read. Today we see the motivational dynamics that have evolved through decades of cultivating an image of the enemy. Obviously a new era has dawned, leaving politicians perplexed and uncertain of themselves.

President Bush took a stand at a relatively early date, July 17, 1989. After the World Economic Summit in Paris, which coincided with the bicentennial of the French Revolution, he gave a speech at the Cathedral of Leyden, Holland, in the presence of the Dutch royal couple. On this occasion the American president stated that we now had the possibility of ending the division of Europe and that we ought to take advantage of our opportunity. He referred to the letter that Mikhail Gorbachev sent to the seven participants of the world economic summit that had convened in Paris on July 14. President Bush's speech in Leyden seems to have symbolically documented the processes whereby in this century, which is known as the American Century, Europe's geographical and historical unity was cut in half by two horrifying wars with more than 60 million dead.

The roots of World War I go back to the exaggerated prestige needs of the nineteenth-century European nation-states. Germany's adversaries eventually asked the United States for help since they were too greatly weakened to achieve victory by themselves. In 1919, despite the good intentions of President Woodrow Wilson and his Fourteen Points, the peace settlement in Europe not only ignored political and ethnic realities but offered no chance for a permanent peace on this continent. Hitler, also a product of the Treaty of Versailles, had no trouble winning over the masses in order to overcome the "humiliation" inflicted upon them. A second world war was merely a question of time—time for the rearming of Germany. Once again the United States had to step in and win the victory of democracy.

In the spring of 1945, President Franklin D. Roosevelt, who was seriously ill, allowed Joseph Stalin to talk him into dividing Europe into a Soviet and an American zone of influence. This guaranteed Russian domination of Eastern Europe from the Bug to the Elbe rivers. We cannot deny that Wilson and Roosevelt, the two American presidents who determined the fate of their country at the end of a world war, had the finest objectives for Europe. But because both men lacked the necessary experience and the precise knowledge of Europe's history and ethnic structures, they were unable to make the correct decisions. This is not meant as a reproach aimed at the United States. It would be more fitting to criticize Europeans themselves; they are chiefly to blame for their terrible quandary, which they brought on themselves through two bloody, internecine conflicts within a century.

The autumn of 1989 introduced a seemingly improbable revolutionary change in the European conditions created by World War II. After seventy-five years of biding its time, Europe is now faced with the historic task of completely overhauling its political and military power structure—the task, as President Bush has phrased it, of ending the division of the continent. As far back as 1946, Winston Churchill, in a memorable speech given in Zurich, spoke about the "United States of Europe" as if he were intent on correcting the blunder that had been carried out in Yalta a year earlier. (In 1956, I took part in the ceremony at Aachen's Coronation Hall when the Charlemagne Prize was awarded to Winston Churchill for his postwar efforts on behalf of European unification.) Charles de Gaulle foresaw a "Europe from the Atlantic to the Urals." Mikhail Gorbachev talks about the "European House" and François Mitterand about the "European Confederation." These concepts, whose very range indicates the breadth and depth of this fascinating restructuring, are all based on an "unknown factor": What role can, should, and will the Soviet Union play in the new Europe?

In the West, Europe's natural frontier is the Atlantic. In the East, it cannot be Poland's eastern border, especially since this demarcation was drawn only recently. Making the Urals the eastern boundary would merely be a display of our high school geography knowledge. My conversations with the Soviet Union taught me that they disagreed with the view of the Urals as Europe's eastern boundary. The Russian Socialist Federative Soviet Republic, the largest in the Union, stretches all the way to Vladivostok. Its new leader, Boris Yeltsin, would certainly oppose any division of his realm by a European border running along the Urals.

I would therefore suggest that Europe's eastern border should not be fixed for the time being. Let the issue remain open for now, especially since we are seeking close economic cooperation across borders and—at least in the West—achieving supranational political integration. Fixing borders would be a throwback to the nation-state thinking of the nineteenth century. I do see, however, the danger of an eastern "border of prosperity" if the unification of the two German states raises the East German living standard to a West European level, while Poland and the Soviet Union have a much harder time offering their people a halfway adequate existence.

How able and willing is Moscow to participate in Europe's unification process? After all, the Soviet Union is not only a global power, it is also a major European power. It still maintains its unrestricted role as one of the victors of 1945, with all the attendant rights and duties in regard to Germany. But we should also recognize that Moscow has an important part to play in a continuing rapprochement between the two halves of Europe— no matter how long and arduous this process may be. We know that the Soviet Union, whose might we have felt threatened by for decades, is changing at a breathtaking pace. In the spring of 1990 the omnipotent Soviet Communist Party was stripped of its power monopoly, thereby forfeiting its position. This loss fore-shadows the spectrum of a multiparty system. Executive author-ity has shifted from the Party to the state—namely, to the newly created presidential position that is vested with a broad mandate.

No one can predict what effect this process of restructuring, indeed dissolution, will have on the overall Soviet picture. De-mands were made for changing the Soviet constitution even before the three Baltic republics launched into their daring seces-sion efforts. Boris Yeltsin has not ruled out a similar path for the Russian Federation. If Russia leaves the Union, then it will be followed by the Ukraine. What will then become of the Trans-Caucasian and Asiatic republics? According to my observations and to statements made by Soviet constitutional experts such as Professor Boguslavski and Dr. Lisitsyn-Svetlanov, the only answer would seem to be a federal restructuring of the Union with greater independence for the individual republics, if only because of the nationalities. But can such a loose association be achieved without the kind of civil-war-like convulsions that have been racking the Caucasus for months now? They could then lead inevitably to an overall collapse. Gorbachev is intent on saving the Union by deferring to the tenets of Lenin, the founder of the Soviet state. The Constitution of the Union of Soviet Socialist Republics, promulgated in 1924, called for a federal state that respected the principle of the nationalities. But Stalin and his successors managed to prevent this, heading off any realization of this idea. After all the cruel experiences with a centralized and cynical dictatorship, the question remains whether the ethnic groups in today's Soviet Union could accept such a constitutional restructuring.

Meanwhile, this trend has become a reality. In July 1990, I had a conversation with Ivan S. Zilayev, who had just been appointed premier of the Russian Federation. I have known him for a long time because as deputy premier of the Soviet government he was in charge of relations with the two German states. Zilayev explained to me that there was no intention of repeated confrontations with the Soviet government because the Soviet constitutional system was going to be discussed in the autumn of 1990 on the basis of a reformulation of the relationship of the various Soviet republics to the central government. It has been proposed that different types of extensive autonomy be granted to the individual republics. According to Zilayev, the Baltic republics could be given the status of a *con*federation, while other republics, especially Russian, would be accorded the status of a federation. On the other hand, the southern republics, especially the Central Asian ones, would have closer ties to the central authorities. The partially autonomous republics would delegate specific powers to the central government, including policies on defense, energy, and currency. I agreed with Mr. Zilayev that the overall disintegration that has been obvious for some time now urgently dictates a swift ratification of this new constitution. The urgency of this particular problem has become evident as the Ukraine and the Byelorussian republic declared independence in July of 1990.

As an economist and banker, I once cited an example from my professional life when discussing the problems of decentralization with my Soviet counterparts. I brought up the organizational and leadership structure of a major industrial corporation with a number of subsidiaries. Each subsidiary, I explained, has its own program; it has to market its products, and its management has full responsibility. The top executives who head the corporation merely assign priorities and resources. The individual subsidiary has to account to those top executives for the results of its actions. By specifically delegating responsibility, the corporation creates latitude for individual initiative, for the creation of an individual image and identification with the job. The individual does not feel like a robot carrying out orders from a remote central office that has little sense of the local conditions.

Granted, my analogy was not quite accurate. Its sole purpose was to make my interlocutors understand what the delegation of authority is all about. But once again I was forced to see how difficult it is to induce even talented and open-minded leaders to abandon stodgy ways of thinking that they take for granted.

The road to transformation of the inner self requires a great deal of patience. The anxiety that the development may spin out of control is quite justified. Russians also fear that Communism may be replaced by a militant nationalism that would release destructive forces to threaten them. Nihilistic and anarchist traits in the Russian mentality were noticeable in earlier times of irritation and uncertainty. The Russian word for this elementary force, which could end in almost masochistic self-destruction, is *stikhinost.* History offers more than enough examples. One was the demonstration at Red Square on May 1, 1990, that turned into an open provocation of government power. I visited Moscow in the spring of 1990, and in a few streets I noticed offensive caricatures of Gorbachev that would have been inconceivable even in the broad-minded West.

Has Gorbachev slackened the reins for too long? Has he relied too strongly on a gradual development of democratic forms and a rational acclimatization to greater freedom? After decades of tight control and brutal exercise of power, this sudden measure of freedom is obviously difficult to digest. The pendulum is swinging in the other direction. Crime has risen to shocking heights. Corruption has always existed here, more or less openly, but today theft, embezzlement, extortion, vandalism of public property, and all kinds of violence are the order of the day. It gives you pause when you are warned (as in New York or São Paulo) against going to unsavory neighborhoods after dark. Recalling my earlier Soviet trips, I realized the great extent that public order has collapsed in this country.

In his newly created office of president of the Soviet Union, Gorbachev has a wealth of powers that none of his forerunners, even Stalin, possessed. The population expects Gorbachev to use his mandate to prevent abuses by calling out the police, in line with Russian tradition, without regard to the possible damage to the first timid stirrings of human rights for Soviet citizens.

With bitter sarcasm a Moscow acquaintance told me that it reminded him of a protocol habit of czarist days: "Whenever the czar approached a *muzhik* [peasant], the latter would kneel down before the divinely ordained ruler and kiss his boots. By way of gratitude the czar would place his foot on the *muzhik*'s neck and, if he felt like it, give him a swat with his whip. The *muzhik* was glad. He knew that the czar was his master, who told him what to do and what not to do. 'He punishes me when I deserve it, and he takes care of me when I need it. I am under his protection.' " As a result, my Moscow acquaintance went on, old Russia had a master-servant hierarchy that was accepted as natural. To him, it satisfied an existential need in Russians, who felt safe as subjects of the czar. In 1862, when Russia abolished serfdom—even before the United States abolished slavery!—many peasants, it is said, begged their masters to allow them to remain with them so that they could continue to receive the orders that were best for them and their families. According to my acquaintance, today's new "call for law and order" shows how strongly rooted that mentality still is.

The unstable situation in the Soviet Union is also triggering other reactions. The Communist Party, deprived of its power monopoly, alleges that the precarious conditions are due chiefly to the fact that the Party can no longer carry out its function as the central force for maintaining order. As a result, the Party is demanding the restoration of its older powers; and its claims are being endorsed by those who believe that this is the only way they can preserve their privileges. Such a demand could certainly find willing listeners. If the general dissolution of public order continues, then the now-scorned Party might gain popularity among the masses, especially because of what they view as the shortcoming of glasnost and perestroika—the lack of law and order.

In short, the Soviet Union needs a new political structure—indeed, a new overall identity. The Soviets will lean more and more in this direction as the widely feared wave of nationalist uprisings in outlying areas keeps spreading. After periods of disturbances and attempted secessions, the individual regions will soon realize that they need to be part of the whole union if only for reasons of economics and security. A federal constitution can then guarantee their individual existence. One can look to West Germany, the United States, and Switzerland as useful examples. Another possibility would be a loose association of states with a more representative than executive leadership, akin to the British Commonwealth. I tend to doubt that this model would be suitable for the Soviet republics, nor can I imagine that President Gorbachev would be satisfied with a mere figurehead role. The Kremlin is not and never will be Buckingham Palace. On the other hand, as the Baltic republics correctly point out, they became part of the Soviet Union only unwillingly: The historical fact is that they were simply annexed. For them, one could envision an economic association for certain practical purposes.

After this turbulent phase of seeking and finding themselves which could lead to overemphasizing regional and ethnic autonomy, the diverse Soviet regions will again attain their freedom of action. The various national groups could then be able to come together in a federal Soviet Union. Perhaps the future Soviet Union will soon opt for the "road to Europe" by choosing gradual integration, moving closer to the cooperating European states, and joining the "European Union." This would have a desirable symbolic effect, for the moment, without grave political consequences.

In the Soviet heartland, the Russian Socialist Federative Soviet Republic, there are also nationalist strivings. Some people are even calling for Russia's complete secession from the Soviet Union. In May 1990 this demand was voiced by Boris Yeltsin, who garnered plaudits—but also stiff opposition from Gorbachev. Yeltsin is exploiting the popular wave of dissatisfaction to promote himself as a super-reformer and as Gorbachev's adversary. He has criticized the methods used by Moscow's central authori-

ties, saying they are the long route to full independence for the
republics. The same question is being asked in both Moscow and
outside the Soviet Union: Can Gorbachev and Yeltsin come to
terms on a reform course?

Amid numerous alarming developments in the Soviet realm,
there are also positive signs that generally elude foreign eyes.
People who wish to embark on a process of renewal and improve
the situation of their country are banding together in most of the
large cities all the way to Siberia. After the regional elections in
March 1990, this trend grew markedly stronger. An efficient communications network, with the goal of carrying out the most
urgent reforms, spread from city to city.

In May and in July 1990 I had a lively exchange of views with
Sergei B. Stankevich, one of the most prominent representatives
of this movement. I am told that this thirty-six-year-old, who was
elected deputy mayor of Moscow in March 1990, is *the* political
mind in Moscow's municipal council. His influence allegedly
extends far into the country. When Stankevich expounded his
ideas about the political overhaul of the Soviet Union, I felt that
this was not a firebrand but a sober-minded person with a deep
political commitment. Stankevich regards the formation of multiple political parties as indispensable. The position of national
president—that is, Gorbachev—should be neutral and nonparti-
san.

A Soviet de Gaulle or a Soviet von Weizsäcker? A man who,
as the supreme referee in the conflict of opinions, as the con-
science of the nation, as the representative of the sovereignty of
the Soviet Union, virtually stands above the pettiness of partisan
wranglings? This possibility is still a long way off, and there is no
telling whether Gorbachev can reach this height. At least one
rival—and tomorrow perhaps two or three—will contest his claim
to exclusivity.

A Frenchman once told me, "The Soviet Union is no longer a
threat to the West, it is a problem. And that may be worse."

Unlike the Chinese leaders, Gorbachev realized at an early

point that economic reforms must be accompanied by social reforms. The creative and productive worker he demands for the
economy does not discard his critical mind at the factory exit. Yet
it was precisely this schizophrenia that the Chinese government
believed it could demand from its citizens. The result was the
drama of June 1989 in Tienanmen Square.

So far Gorbachev has managed to forestall such developments
in his country. But while the economic reforms bog down, the
social reforms are advancing at breakneck speed. This deepening
split is highly explosive. The moment of truth has arrived, bringing with it realistic pricing. The man at the top has no choice but
to appeal to reason . . . or resort to violence?

Within the Party, Gorbachev, by means of liberal domination,
has managed to field the increasingly open and contentious debate. The 1989 election for the Congress of People's Deputies was
the first one in which rival candidates ran against one another;
and the sessions of the congress, witnessed by a global audience,
became a broad forum for free speech.

The ethnic autonomy strivings have had a sobering effect. They
prove that a timid decentralizing is not enough to satisfy the
rebellious nations of the Soviet Union, which is made up of over
a hundred ethnic groups. The Soviet leadership will have to recognize that this country can be held together only by a resolutely
federal structure that can protect the often small ethnic groups
against their neighbors and especially against being swallowed up
by the Russians, who form the largest nationality. In this enormous land, democracy and federalism are Siamese twins. In June
1989, I discussed this view with Professor Vladimir Shenayev,
deputy director of the European Institute of the Soviet Academy
of Sciences. He agreed with me in theory.

No less serious are the social conflicts vented in wildcat strikes
and walkouts inundating the entire country. This phenomenon
is not linked to any one system. The transition from dictatorship
to democracy in other countries—Greece, Spain, South America,
and so on—has also been accompanied by labor struggles. The

waters of the new freedom have to be tested. Outbursts are inevitable, especially after decades of social abuse enforced by the threat of violence. But such excesses aggravate the supply crisis, prompting not only orthodox Party members but also ordinary citizens to call for a firm hand.

A further source of conservative backlash is to be feared. The officials stripped of their privileges could rebel, the economically disadvantaged could rise up, and the victims of the social situation could offer resistance. If the earlier division of powers had been upheld, then the Central Committee or the politburo might have eventually put an end to the Party chief's reform zeal, initiating a phase of stagnation. But both these once-so-mighty institutions of the Communist Party were deliberately shunted aside. The newly elected Soviet president probably cannot be dethroned without decisive involvement by the Supreme Soviet and the Congress of People's Deputies. An interesting question remains: To what extent will the newly established Presidential Council, which still has to be constitutionally approved, be assigned a meaningful role? This needs to be resolved with a view toward securing the state leadership. Sober and serious forecasts about the further development of the Soviet Union seem impossible against this turbulent background. History teaches us that developments do not run in a straight line; leaps, breaks, and reversals are the rule rather than the exception. Gorbachev was able to get a majority support only because Andropov was followed by Chernenko. The stagnation, indeed regression, became obvious after a brief period of relief under Andropov.

Perhaps the lumbering colossus of the Soviet Union needs to take another step back in order to carry out a third, more decisive and universally accepted push for liberal reform and actual restructuring. This would mean that the new order can emerge only after the old system has collapsed. But the restructuring is as certain as the current setbacks.

No one can or will seriously deny the extremely precarious situation of this enormous country after seventy years of centralized economic planning. The infrastructure of thinking is negative and therefore unsuitable for a quick conversion of reform ideas into reality—even though this may be the only chance for improvement. The country and its people will have to go through a long and hard purgatory. And any successor to the current president could also not afford to ignore these deep-rooted and politically dangerous abuses, which have now been exposed for all to see.

The Soviet Union, which is the largest country on this planet, has gigantic deposits of natural resources that have not been efficiently exploited if at all. It also has a considerable natural reserve in labor and intelligence, but this is no developing country in the conventional sense. It possesses biological and material reserves; its scientific, especially technological, achievements are brilliant; and it combines a high cultural standard with a historically developed self-assurance. Numerous talks with outstanding representatives of those fields—under Leonid Brezhnev and even now—have confirmed my view that the Soviet Union would accept assistance from the West only as a partner and on the basis of full parity. Patronizing recommendations as to what must or could be done have, understandably, only caused irritation.

We Germans have a special part to play in giving Moscow the assistance it wants. From the time of Peter the Great (whom the Soviets, maintaining a certain aloofness, call Peter I) until the Revolution of 1917, the czarist empire was served by Germans from all walks of life. Many Russians still realize this, if only subconsciously. For two centuries Germans left their imprint on Russia: in the urban bourgeoisie, in the imperial courts and armies—in which the Baltic aristocracy had a dominant position— and among farmers in the remote provinces. After all, since the days of Catherine the Great, German settlers reclaimed vast areas, making them arable and productive. The German who helps in a time of need is a traditional figure in Russian culture. He was there when he was needed.

In 1859, Goncharov immortalized him in his amusing novel

Oblomov. Oblomov, a member of the lower Russian aristocracy, is likable and amiable but lacks resolve. Whenever he has trouble organizing something, he can always count on his friend Stolz, who is of German descent. Here is a characteristic conversation:

"Sooner or later you'll have to stop working," Oblomov remarked.

"I'll never stop. Why should I?"

"When you've doubled your capital," said Oblomov.

"I won't stop even if I quadruple it."

"Why do you have to drudge like that," Oblomov went on after a pause, "if your goal is not to establish lifelong security and then retire and breathe a sigh of relief . . ."

"Rustic Oblomovism," Stolz exclaimed.

". . . or attain prestige and a social position by means of a government post and enjoy your well-deserved rest and honorable leisure?"

"Petersburg Oblomovism!"

"Then when do you intend to live?" Oblomov retorted angrily. "Why drudge your whole life away?"

This novel is evidently popular in the Soviet Union. During a confidential meeting about problems with our collaboration, a Soviet participant, alluding to this historical experience, cried out to me: "We simply need an Ivan Stolz!"

In 1918, Lenin urged his comrades: "Learn from the Germans!" And during the 1920s, Foreign Trade Minister Leonid Krasin stated: "Russia and Germany were made for each other." I have detected similar attitudes during many conversations with Russians.

But the lessons the Russians learned from horrible historical experiences with the Germans remain entrenched. The West European, especially the West German, asks, Why did Moscow under Khrushchev and Brezhnev pursue such mammoth armaments policies? For decades they were the uppermost priority of the Soviets, who apparently placed no limits on human and material expenditures. To top it off, these efforts were incomprehensible because the balance of power made any threat of danger from the West unrealistic. We found no rational basis for Moscow's hypersensitive security needs.

In my opinion the roots are to be found in a kind of trauma, which cannot be explained by reciting mere numbers. During conversations in which we were frank enough to broach delicate issues, I kept hearing the same thing over and over: Despite the vehement Soviet attitude toward Hitlerism, the German Wehrmacht made a profound impact on the Russians during the Great Patriotic War. A later effect of this experience is the high prestige that West Germany's Bundeswehr enjoys within the NATO forces even if its army is to be reduced in the future.

What the Soviets appreciate most about the Germans is something they feel they do not have: organizational talent. The Russian inability to react swiftly to unforeseeable disasters was demonstrated in Chernobyl in 1986 and after the Armenian earthquake in December 1988. On the other hand, the Russians are very good at improvising.

German soldiers will no doubt remember the Russians' phenomenal knack for dealing with combat problems or with a lack of weapons and equipment. We were constantly amazed by "Ivan's" resourcefulness in critical situations.

I will always remember with gratitude how willing my interlocutors were to open up after both sides had patiently suffered through the ideological clichés, but I am also cautious. When speaking about the historical impact of Germans on Russia, I must point out that the occasionally powerful German influence, especially on the politics of the czarist court, also became a nuisance. One backlash was the Slavic national movement around the turn of the century, which disrupted for a long time the good rapport between Russians and Germans. We must always keep this experience in mind whenever we offer to help the Soviet Union.

Nor should we forget the impact of this development on our

Western neighbors who have a thin skin whenever German foreign policy heads toward closer bonds with Moscow. Europeans
are quick to bring up Tauroggen and Rapallo.*

Today we are heading toward a Europe that is going to move
closer together both economically and politically as of 1993.
Should we not start thinking about some kind of European division of labor within the framework of international cooperation?
A list of priorities could be set up: The British might be in charge
of relations with their American cousin, the French and Italians
with their African neighbors, the Spanish and Portuguese with
their descendants in Latin America. The fundamental overhaul in
Eastern Europe is confronting the Germans with a new situation.
I do not doubt that a united Germany—after solving the overwhelming social and material problems of its reunification—will
focus not only on Central and Western Europe but also on the
Soviet Union. This will involve increasingly larger burdens
before any economic gains are realized. A "European" mandate
to avoid misunderstandings would be urgently needed. We
should continue to ask our Common Market neighbors and the
United States to assist us by, say, forming European banking and
industrial syndicates. For centuries France has maintained a close
rapport with Poland and Rumania, and this should be respected.
Its overall structure would, from the very outset, exclude any
German solo approach to Eastern Europe. Furthermore, the Eastern European policies of this plan would not be a national undertaking in the classical imperialistic sense; instead, it would consist
of an array of supranational European tasks. Ultimately, the
United States would also have to be included.

Can the lessons of the past be of any help? History cannot be
mathematically analyzed. Ideas and people create imponderables,
while chance, indeed paradox, has often determined historical
events. Was it not an imperial, capitalist Germany that helped
Lenin and his Bolsheviks attain their victory? Is it not paradoxical

---

* See notes on pp. 141 and xi.

that seventy years after the October Revolution, Gorbachev is trying to force a "catch-up" revolution from above in order to achieve the goals that the French bourgeoisie was pursuing two centuries ago? In the eyes of orthodox Marxists, the French Revolution was never anything but a bourgeois revolt against despotism, actions to cement the power of the ruling class. And now all at once an enlightened Soviet socialism is trying to bring about human rights, a constitutional state, freedom of assembly, and freedom of speech.

We can only hope that the Kremlin bastille will not be stormed. In their philosophical significance, the revolutionary factors in the current Soviet development are the radical change of the consciousness of the people, the irreversibility of the route being taken, the collapse of the old ideology. Revolution is never merely destruction, it also contains the seeds of a new order; Gorbachev himself has decreed the second Soviet revolution from above—a revolution that also aims at dismantling the old infrastructures of society, economy, and thinking in order to erect the future on their remains.

Fyodor Dostoevsky saw Russia as a young nation that was only just starting to live. Is Russia throwing off the shackles of centuries of fatalism and developing its tremendous dormant powers, which are enabling it to charge into the "European Century"?

In France, human rights, tested by the French Revolution, experienced many twists and turns before establishing themselves as the core of the state doctrine. Will the Soviet Union go through a similar cycle? A return to rigid Party domination and to a silencing of the population seems improbable. The superiority of a free system with an institutional framework based on democracy and on the market economy has became far too obvious; its enormous economic potential can no longer be denied. A highly developed satellite technology guarantees instant global communication around the globe, making the sequestering of information impossible.

For decades capitalism and Marxism were embroiled in a bitter rivalry. Now the fight has been won. One could say (somewhat overstating the case): While in the past obsolete propertied classes caused revolutions, in the future the sophisticated world-wide communications systems will shatter the old structures. The systems of Rumania, Czechoslovakia, East Germany, and even Albania had no hope of survival in a world with global communications. Viewed retrospectively, the historical development is consistent, and yet we seemed to be a long way from the time when the final islands of dictatorship would vanish from our Europe. Our century is termed the "American Century," but it has also been branded by an inhumane Communism that captured nations and held them in bondage behind an Iron Curtain. However, "freedom" is what Mikhail Gorbachev keeps claiming for the Soviet people; it was documented in the Bonn Declaration of June 13, 1989.

We are about to enter the third millennium. The twentieth century, one of the most gruesome in human history with over 60 million dead in two world wars and countless others in subsequent conflicts, will be behind us in just a few years. A new millennium exerts a powerful suggestive effect on people. Are we truly facing a new era? Will this be the first time in human memory that we do not have to fear for any new war for future generations?

Our expectations are justified. There are signs of changes in world events, signs that were inconceivable until very recently. The balance of power between the two military blocs once appeared so solid; now the Eastern half containing the terror seems to have perished. Long-familiar absolutes and fixed positions are shifting, becoming relative; they are no longer suitable for the interplay of forces. Everyone is talking to everyone else.

NATO has long been moving toward political rather than military methods as the first resort. This approach can succeed only if we include the Soviet Union in our plans; that is, take their legitimate security interests into account. Let us not forget that Moscow has had to give up its *cordon sanitaire*—primarily Poland and East Germany—which it has obstinately defended for decades. Nor should we ignore the dangers besetting the domestic cohesion of the Soviet Union. This is a highly sensitive issue that must be handled sensitively.

In June 1990, President Bush and President Gorbachev met for a summit meeting in Washington. It was assumed that a pan-European security plan had to be developed before Moscow would permit a united Germany to join NATO. Imagine the demands being made on Moscow: Not only does the Soviet superpower have to admit to itself that it has lost the Cold War, but now regarding this NATO issue it has to face the realization that it cannot hold on to the trophies of World War II. For decades Soviet propaganda has portrayed NATO as the dreaded arch-foe; but now the Soviet population has to be convincingly shown that NATO is taking cogent steps to assure peace. The declaration made at the NATO summit during July 1990 evinced a surprising unanimity in initiating these steps. Manfred Wörner, secretary general of NATO, went to the Kremlin and personally elucidated these plans to President Gorbachev; he then invited him to visit NATO headquarters and express his opinion to their assembly. Unexpected cooperation has emerged. After the welter of multinational conferences and the twenty-eighth Congress of the Communist Party, at which Gorbachev managed to gain a precarious but still sufficient latitude, he and Helmut Kohl engaged in bilateral talks during mid-July 1990. The results were surprising. Moscow will allow a united Germany to join NATO; by granting the Germans full sovereignty, Moscow is opening the gates for a unified foreign policy for Germany. In return, Germany will provide the Soviets with comprehensive economic aid and support. The superpowers have come to realize that they cannot act alone in solving conflicts militarily or politically—whether in the Middle East or in their own backyards such as Afghanistan and Nicaragua. This insight is fostering mutual understanding. Indeed, the awareness of their interdependence is supplanting foreign policies based on "containment" and military superiority.

On the other hand, China's role in global affairs remains an unpredictable factor for both sides. And just as the danger of war in the East-West relationship is diminishing, regional conflicts are growing in number and intensity; on this level, East-West ideological antagonism has been replaced by ethnic and religious friction and disputes over resources.

Nevertheless, five decades of nonwar can now give way to a phase of active peacemaking. The Soviet and Western governments have clearly declared their intention to proceed on that course, as evidenced by the U.S.–Soviet cooperation in August 1990 in connection with the conflict over Kuwait.

In his country Gorbachev is working on the foundation of a new Soviet house while already thinking about the European house. But the new structure is still fragile. It could be swept away by any storm—such as the one that blasted across Beijing's Square of Heavenly Peace.

Except for archconservatives and comfortable officeholders, nobody questions the need for radical reforms; it is the pace and the methods that are being hotly debated. Supposedly Gorbachev grossly underestimated the time factor and the behavior of the disparate ethnic groups, especially in view of the deteriorating supply situation. Yeltsin and his followers are demanding a faster tempo and even more radical action. Moving in between is the broad spectrum of critics and know-it-alls.

Gorbachev is impatient; he urges, he cajoles and demands, he ceaselessly attacks apathy and sloppiness. And considering the massive abuses he rails against and the fear that the changes are coming too late, we perhaps cannot expect a measured and moderate course of action.

Furthermore, the "new thinking" is triggering not only the desired responses but also unexpected, even uncontrollable ones—such as strikes, unrest—that force their own rhythm on the government.

The Soviet Union is faced with difficult domestic problems. The multinational state requires a federally based constitution, which in turn requires a different view of the state. A new identity has to be found. This is an enormous undertaking, and Gorbachev is embarking on it at a great risk to himself.

Unlike millions of indolent Party members, he feels the vibrations that are announcing the new international system of the coming millennium. He knows the dangers threatening Soviet supremacy and also the opportunities awaiting his gigantic country with its boundless resources. Both realistic and visionary in his outlook, he sees a Soviet Union that has to fight for its place in the steadily growing power triangle made up of Europe, the United States, and the Pacific basin. He realizes that in order to avoid losing its position as a world power, his country must compete successfully with the newest economic giants in both the East and the West; that is, Western Europe and the Pacific basin.

I would advocate helping Gorbachev in these endeavors. By so doing we would be helping everyone: the nations in the Soviet Union, the nations in Asia, the nations in Europe, and our American friends. Dictatorships would be superseded by economic opportunity. If, as Gorbachev promises, this route will lead his people to their lasting freedom and human dignity, then there is no reason that the free world should not lend him a hand. His political fate is also contingent on whether the Soviet nations wish to join him in taking the thorny road to new destinations while patiently enduring all sorts of deprivation.

None of us has any reason to be smug. In the future all our strength and attention will be taxed by natural disasters, hatred between nations, religious fanaticism, as well as worldwide ecological problems and, last but not least, epidemics such as AIDS and the escalating global catastrophe of drug addiction. The German unification process will likewise make its demands on us for a long time. Nor can we forget our contribution to solving the plight of the Third World, especially black Africa and Latin America. They are pinning their hopes on us.

As the German historian Leopold von Ranke said, "Every nation is equally close to and far from God." We are neither smarter nor fairer nor more moral than our ancestors, but our century has experienced greater misfortune and destruction than earlier ones. This prompts us to hope that the horrors may have taught us how to attain an irreversible peace on this planet.

We have come to the home stretch of this century, which has been so fateful for Europe. The final decade before the start of the next millennium is giving us a chance to lay the foundation for a united and peaceful Europe, which we may be able to achieve in the next century. The growth of worldwide communication, which knows no national borders, and the impact of a new era allow us to hope that all human beings will cooperate in implementing the new geopolitical vision now offered to us.

More than anything else, we have to cast off the traditional national structures. The European Economic Community has set out on this course, which will eventually affect the other European countries. The Eastern European countries, having long been deprived of self-determination, are urgently intent on emphasizing their inviolable borders. But ultimately they will have to yield, slowly but ineluctably, to the global lifting of such demarcations. Europe's future—and that of the Eastern European nations—can only lie within a supraregional European organization with a considerable economic strength. Only an open society with the greatest possible freedom for its citizens can tackle the imminent social tasks, enabling us to live in harmony with our environment. A federal constitution addresses the special needs of regions and nations, thereby providing room for individuality; this is the only way in which to appeal to the individual, making him part of the political structure and arousing his allegiance. Economy and ecology also require vast cooperation that transcends national borders.

In the course of mutual give and take, the West will remember the spiritual and cultural values of the East. Despite the anomaly of the divided continent, the West has a favorable climate for economic growth and prosperity. Broad segments of the population that have grown accustomed to these advantages are increasingly saturated, and postindustrial society is stressing new developments. State-of-the-art products and external comforts are not enough to satisfy people. For some time now the mentality of the Euro-American consumer society has made us forget that the West and the East are linked in a common destiny. Millions of people on the other side of the Iron Curtain need our advice and our material help for revamping their economy, their society, and their political structure. After decades of East European purgatory, which we West Europeans were spared, we will be enriched by the cultural and moral substance of the citizens in the Eastern part of our continent. We are rediscovering a Russia that was estranged from us by years of confrontation and forced isolation. Europe's nations were deprived of the experience of a shared history and culture; attitudes in the Communist nations were deformed, distorted. But Dostoevsky already taught us about the spiritual strength of these people, which has never been broken, despite the lack of freedom in czarist and Soviet times. Their material plight notwithstanding, this strength is a rich heritage— a rich gift to a "European Union," fortifying us in our quest for postmaterial values.

The end of this development will be a united Europe, flanked on the East and on the West by the two superpowers: the United States, within the framework of NATO, and the reformed Soviet Union. But both will no longer have their dominant role as superpowers. Instead, they will function on the basis of parity of the European concept. For a long time now their confrontation has alienated us from our European identity and history; the struggle between the interests of the superpowers was waged over our heads, and we feared losing our self-determination forever. Let us benefit from history's offer and find ourselves by means of responsible creative endeavors.

Above all the Soviet Union, confronted as it is with tremendous internal upheavals, has to maintain its full ability to function in the international arena. This is the only possibility of success for Europe's restructuring. This closes the circle between the NATO summit in London, with its constructive security proposals, the Dublin conference of the EEC leaders, and the Houston conference, which, chaired by President Bush, agreed on joint assistance for the Soviet recovery process. The goal that has been set will be reached only if the huge Soviet Union can settle its chaotic economy and solve the supply problems. In turn, this can happen only with massive Western assistance.

By June 1990, West Germany had already taken steps in this direction by granting Moscow a loan of 5 billion marks with no strings attached. For West Germany, which has long been the Soviet Union's most important Western trading partner, this was the right move at the right time. But more must be done. Significant as the German contribution is, we cannot overlook the fact that tomorrow's Germany cannot be the only country dealing with Soviet difficulties. Moreover, for political reasons a long-term Western plan that includes all aspects of Soviet economic recovery is not only desirable but indispensable. This would be the best approach to maintaining a compatible balance of influence by Western industrial nations. No ad hoc activity, however well-meaning, can solve this complex problem.

Such a recovery plan should not be foisted upon a world power like the Soviet Union. We should respect its pride. We should jointly develop and implement this plan on the basis of cooperative parity. Moscow and the Western countries should talk about and agree on methods that will observe the time frame and the priorities, leaving room for necessary adjustments as each phase is enacted under joint control by the participants. Credits would then have conditions but no one-sided ones; linked to specific projects, they would help to execute the program that has been mutually worked out. By the same token, Moscow would have to grant investment and market opportunities to Western industry—that is, private capital—and West European markets would have to be open to Soviet exports with higher profit margins and not just raw materials. The entire concept is a great challenge that can succeed only by means of an extensive division of labor among international institutions—for example, the European Economic Community administration in Brussels and the International Monetary Fund, which can also assist in the gradual process of making the ruble convertible. The Bank for East European Reconstruction, which is in the process of being established, involves not only the European nations, including the Soviet Union, but also the United States; eventually it could take over the task of coordination.

Mikhail Gorbachev is not the only one who has grossly underestimated the problems of perestroika in regard to the Soviet Union. We must learn as well. Even though the Russians have to deal with their own domestic problems, we should realize that the West, for its own sake, must soberly figure out how it can help if we are not to lose this historic chance of a restructuring for the entire European continent.

IMPORTANT DATES

Vladimir Ilyich Lenin	1870–1924
Leon Trotsky	1879–1940
Joseph Stalin	1879–1953
Czar Nicholas II dethroned	March 1917
October Revolution	October–November 1917
Separate Peace of Brest Litovsk (Germany and Russia)	March 3, 1918
The New Economic Policy	1921–28
Treaty of Rapallo with Germany	April 16, 1922
Founding of the Soviet Union	December 30, 1922
Beginning of forced collectivization, fight against the Kulaks	January 1928
Annexation of the Baltic states	October 1939
Hitler's invasion of the U.S.S.R.	June 22, 1941
The Battle of Moscow	October–December 1941
The Battle of Stalingrad	October 1942–February 2, 1943
Teheran Conference	November 28–December 1, 1943
D-day (Allied invasion of Europe)	June 6, 1944
Red Army crosses Polish border	July 4, 1944
Yalta Conference	February 4–12, 1945

Soviets occupy Königsberg	April 16, 1945
Fall of Berlin	May 2, 1945
Potsdam Conference	July 17–August 2, 1945
Berlin Blockade	1948–49
Stalin's death	March 5, 1953
Warsaw Pact	May 14, 1955
Konrad Adenauer in Moscow; diplomatic relations begin between U.S.S.R. and West Germany	September 1955
Twentieth Congress of the Soviet Communist Party (Nikita Khrushchev posthumously topples Stalin)	February 14–25, 1956
Hungarian Uprising	October–November 1956
First Soviet satellite	October 4, 1957
Construction of Berlin Wall	August 13, 1961
Pipeline embargo	1963
Soviet intervention in Czechoslovakia	August 21, 1968
First U.S.-Soviet SALT talks in Helsinki	December 17–22, 1969
First pipeline/gas/credit agreement	February 1, 1970
Soviet–West German nonviolence treaty, recognition of the existing borders in Europe, and normalization of relations (Leonid Brezhnev–Willy Brandt)	August 12, 1970
Four Powers Treaty on Berlin	August 23, 1971
West German Chancellor Willy Brandt in Oreanda, Crimea	September 1971
President Richard Nixon in U.S.S.R., Joint Declaration, ABM Treaty, SALT-1	May 22–30, 1972

East German Constitution, Article 6: GDR allied forever and irrevocably with U.S.S.R.	September 27, 1974
Conference on European Security and Cooperation, final signing in Helsinki	August 1, 1975
SALT II in Vienna, signed by Brezhnev and Jimmy Carter	June 15–16, 1979
NATO double resolution	December 12, 1979
Soviet troops occupy Afghanistan; U.S.S.R. cites Soviet-Afghanistan agreement	December 27, 1979
Strikes in Poland (Gdansk, Szczecin)	August 1980
Central Committee plenary session: meat and milk shortages, Gorbachev (born March 2, 1931) appointed to the politburo	October 21, 1980
Premier Alexei Kosygin resigns; succeeded by Nikolai Tikhonov	October 22, 1980
Tenth congress of the Soviet-German Economic Commission: gas/pipeline deal	September 24–28, 1981
Brezhnev in *Spiegel* interview: Europe, the frailest of all human houses	November 2, 1981
U.S.S.R. begins to supply gas to West Germany	November 20, 1981
Brezhnev visits Bonn, Schmidt: comprehensive political security partnership	November 22–25, 1981
INF (Intermediate-range Nuclear Forces) talks begin in Geneva	November 30, 1981
START talks begin in Geneva	June 29, 1982

Yamal pipeline agreement signed in Leningrad	July 1982
Brezhnev dies	October 10, 1982
Yuri Andropov becomes general secretary	October 12, 1982
South Korean passenger plane shot down over Soviet territory, 269 dead	September 1, 1983
Andropov dies	February 9, 1984
Konstantin Chernenko elected general secretary	February 13, 1984
Amur-Baikal-Magistrale railroad line opened after ten years' construction	November 7, 1984
Chernenko dies	March 10, 1985
Mikhail Gorbachev elected general secretary	March 11, 1985
Warsaw Pact summit meeting in Warsaw; pact extended twenty years	April 26, 1985
Premier Tikhonov resigns; succeeded by Nikolai Ryzhkov	September 27, 1985
Reagan-Gorbachev summit in Geneva	November 19–21, 1985
Viktor Grishin, the Moscow Party chief, replaced by Boris Yeltsin	December 24, 1985
Gorbachev proposes complete nuclear disarmament by the year 2000	January 15, 1986
1:23 A.M., accident at Chernobyl nuclear plant near Kiev	April 26, 1986
Reagan-Gorbachev summit meeting in Reykjavik	October 11–12, 1986
Brezhnev first criticized in *Pravda*	December 19, 1986
Creation of joint Soviet-foreign	December 25, 1986

ventures is approved by
politburo

Peace Congress in Moscow — February 1987

In one region within each of the — June 21, 1987
fifteen Soviet republics, for the
first time, several candidates
run for office in the local
soviets

In his speech in Murmansk, — October 1, 1987
Gorbachev proposes reducing
military activities in Northern
Europe; the Kola Peninsula,
previously off limits, is opened
for collaborations with the
West

Yeltsin replaced as Party chief in — October 21, 1987
Moscow

Gorbachev's book *Perestroika*, — November 1, 1987
with a first printing of 300,000
copies, appears in Soviet
bookshops

Gorbachev's book becomes — November 19, 1987
available in Western countries

Signing of the INF treaty at the — December 8, 1987
third Reagan-Gorbachev
summit meeting, in
Washington

Time magazine names Gorbachev — December 1987
"Man of the Decade"—"a
symbol of hope for a new
Soviet Union"

A new Soviet enterprise law goes — January 1, 1988
into effect, providing for
economical accounting,
self-financing, and individual
responsibility in a business;
unprofitable undertakings will

be shut down. The law applies
to about sixty percent of Soviet
industrial production.

The Zurich Bank for Credit and   January 19–22, 1988
Foreign Trade offers the first
public loan to the Soviet
Union (100 million Swiss
francs) in international money
markets

In Geneva, the foreign ministers   April 14, 1988
of Afghanistan, Pakistan, and
the Soviet Union sign several
agreements on the political
settlement of the Afghanistan
situation, which go into effect
on May 15. The withdrawal of
foreign troops from
Afghanistan is scheduled to
take place in nine months.

Fourth Reagan-Gorbachev summit   May 29–June 2, 1988
meeting, in Moscow

Start of two-week celebration of   June 5, 1988
the millennium of Russia's
christianization. On April 29,
Gorbachev, in a conversation
with Pimen, the patriarch of
Moscow and all Russia,
declares that perestroika also
applies to the Church.

According to a *Tass* bulletin, the   July 30, 1988
Central Committee decides on
a schedule for Gorbachev's
reform plans: By the end of
1988, all 20 million Party
members are to vote on new
Party officials who are to serve
no more than two five-year

terms. The Congress of
People's Deputies is to convene
in the spring of 1989 and
appoint a Soviet president.

At a session of the Supreme   October 1, 1988
Soviet, convened at short
notice, Gorbachev, general
secretary of the Central
Committee of the Soviet
Communist Party, is elected
president of the Supreme
Soviet, thereby becoming head
of the Soviet state

The executive committee of the   October 7, 1988
Supreme Soviet of the Soviet
Republic of Lithuania decrees
that Lithuanian is the official
language of Lithuania

Minister of Finances Boris   October 27, 1988
Gostev, at a meeting of the
Supreme Soviet, submits a
draft of the government budget
for 1989. The budget deficit,
reported for the first time,
constitutes more than seven
percent of the total budget.

A serious earthquake in the   December 7, 1988
Republic of Armenia; the
epicenters are in the cities of
Kirovakan and Leninakan. For
the first time, Moscow appeals
for Western help. Reagan-
Gorbachev summit cut short.

For the first time since 1933 the   February 14, 1989
Soviet Ministry of the Interior
releases Soviet crime statistics

Nationwide Soviet elections for   March 26, 1989

the Congress of People's Deputies. In about seventy-five percent of the fourteen hundred election districts, two or more candidates run for office.	
Starting on April 1, fifty thousand Soviet troops and matériel are to be withdrawn from Hungary, Czechoslovakia, and East Germany (in two phases until the end of 1990)	April 1989
The Supreme Soviet of the Soviet Union issues a government edict permitting long-term leasing of property and equipment, especially land for private and cooperative use (for fifty years or more)	April 8, 1989
Summit meeting between General Secretary Gorbachev and Chinese President Deng Xiaoping in Beijing—the first Soviet-Chinese summit since 1959	May 15–18, 1989
Soviet Congress of People's Deputies meets, decides on Moscow's basic domestic and foreign policies. In an appeal to Soviet citizens, the People's Deputies call for a "humane and democratic Socialism."	May 25–June 24, 1989
Gorbachev visits West Germany	June 12–15, 1989
In a TV speech, Gorbachev, head of the Communist Party and head of state, warns the Soviet	July 1, 1989

population against "stirring up
national emotions."

In the Kusnets basin, the miners   July 10–20, 1989
go on strike to emphasize their
demands for better supplies of
consumer goods and for the
financial independence of the
coal mines in which they
work. By July 14, the strikes
spread throughout the entire
Kusnets basin. Social demands
are then accompanied by
political demands. On July 19,
the strikes spread to mines in
Vorkuta in the north as well as
Donets and Karaganda (in
northern Kazakhstan). On July
20, the miners in the Donetsk
basin go back to work.

In the autonomous territory of   July 10, 1989
Nagorno-Karabakh, additional
strikes last several days

Publication of Gorbachev's   July 15, 1989
welcoming speech to the
participants of the economic
summit in Paris. The Soviet
head of state and Party chief
offers a "constructive dialogue"
about international economic
coordination.

In the autonomous republic of   July 15, 1989
Abkhasia (in the Republic of
Georgia), armed conflicts
between Georgians and
Abkhazians

In his speech, Party chief   July 18, 1989

Gorbachev says that in regard
to the economy, the Central
Committee of the Communist
Party must find a solution for
the situation that has
developed. To overcome the
shortage of goods for daily
needs, all the domestic reserves
would have to be used, plus
additional imports amounting
to 10 billion rubles.

At a plenary session of the   July 19, 1989
Supreme Soviet, Deputy Boris
Yeltsin calls upon the deputies
to participate in the work of a
supraregional group of deputies
reflecting the opinions of
"left-wing–radical segments of
the population"

The Soviet Communist Party   August 17, 1989
publishes the draft of
guidelines for policies on
ethnic groups. The
transformation of the Soviet
Union into a confederation is
rejected; a secession right for
republics is not mentioned.
The Party confirms a strict
adherence to the unified
structure and to "democratic
centralism."

The Supreme Soviet passes a law   October 9, 1989
on "settling labor disputes."
This is the first time that the
possibility of strike is dealt
with in the law.

Erich Honecker, the beleaguered   October 18, 1989

East German head of state and
Communist Party chief, asks to
be relieved of his duties "for
health reasons." The East
German Central Committee, at
the suggestion of the politburo,
unanimously elects Egon Krenz
(secretary of the Central
Committee) the new general
secretary of the Central
Committee of East Germany's
Socialist Unity Party.

Along with Moscow's official   November 7, 1989
military parade celebrating the
seventy-second anniversary of
the October Revolution, a
counter-demonstration by
various oppositional groups is
permitted.

Opening of East Germany's and   November 9, 1989
East Berlin's borders to West
Germany and West Berlin

The Supreme Soviet of the   December 7, 1989
Lithuanian Republic eliminates
the article in the Lithuanian
constitution about the Soviet
Communist Party as "the
leading and guiding force in
Soviet society"

Second Congress of People's   December 12–24, 1989
Deputies, Premier Nikolai
Ryzhkov submits a plan for
the Soviet economic recovery

The Lithuanian Communist   December 19–23, 1989
Party, at its congress, votes to
secede from the Soviet
Communist Party and form an

independent Lithuanian
Communist Party

Working visit of Marian Calfa   December 20, 1989
and Jiri Dienstbier, the premier
and the foreign minister of
Czechoslovakia. Both sides
agree to discuss in the coming
weeks the issue of the Soviet
troops stationed in
Czechoslovakia.

At a mass demonstration in   February 4, 1990
Moscow (according to *Tass:*
two hundred thousand
participants), various speakers
demand the elimination of the
power monopoly of the
Communist Party and a
comprehensive democratization
of state and society

Plenary Congress of the Central   February 5–7, 1990
Committee of the Soviet
Communist Party: elimination
of Article 6 of the Soviet
constitution that establishes
the leadership position of the
Communist Party

West German Chancellor Helmut   February 10–11, 1990
Kohl and Foreign Minister
Hans-Dietrich Genscher meet
with Gorbachev and Soviet
Foreign Minister Eduard
Shevardnadze at short notice
to discuss the latest
developments in the German
issue and its impact on Europe.
According to the official Soviet
information, Gorbachev tells

Kohl that there are no
differences of opinion between
the U.S.S.R., West Germany,
and East Germany about
letting the Germans decide for
themselves on the question of
unity for the German nation
and make their own choices
about the political form and
the conditions of this unity.
This can only happen,
however, within the context of
the overall European
development, and it must take
into account the security and
other interests of their
neighbors and also other
countries in Europe and the
rest of the world.

First free elections for East   March 18, 1990
    Germany's People's Chamber
At the first session of the   March 27, 1990
    Presidential Council,
    Gorbachev advocates a broader
    and faster implementation of
    economic reform
Meeting of the Conference on   April 1990
    European Security and
    Cooperation in Bonn
Chinese Premier Li Peng visits   April 23–26, 1990
    Moscow
Soviet Premier Ryzhkov: May 24, 1990
    "Transition to a regulated
    market economy"
Bush-Gorbachev summit meeting   May 30–June 3, 1990
    in Washington
Agreement on a West German   June 1990

loan of 5 billion deutschmarks
to the Soviet Union

Conference of Common Market   June 25–26, 1990
heads of state and government
in Dublin

Twenty-eighth Congress of the   July 2–13, 1990
Soviet Communist Party

NATO summit meeting in   July 5–6, 1990
London

World economic summit in   July 9–11, 1990
Houston

West German Chancellor Kohl   July 14–16, 1990
visits Gorbachev in Moscow
and Shelesnovodsk